Crossing the Chari River

A Memoir of Perseverance and Joy

by

Joy Klaaren Forgwe Ortiz

Published by Franklin Publishers

Printed in the United States of America

For permissions, inquiries, or additional copies, contact:

Franklin Publishers

www.franklinpublishers.com

Preface

———— ∞ ————

S itting on the cool, breezy banks of Lake Macatawa, I scribbled my jumbled thoughts onto tiny scraps of notebook paper – thoughts obscured by wounds I refused to share. I was a nineteen-year-old college student trying to grasp what had just happened.

My silence festered – collecting even more layers of reticence -- as I yearned to understand what led my first love to turn distant and abusive. But my lips remained as tightly closed as the paper scraps that I had boxed up, sealed, and stored away.

My appetite for love and joy and beauty bounced back to the surface when I became a mother, a vessel for new life. As my children grew into adulthood, my silent-coated past threw me into frustration, despair, and anger.

Fortuitously I came across those sealed boxes I had stored away decades earlier. Attempting to cope with depression and the challenges of parenting four children caught between two worlds, I began journalizing.

As I moved closer to my 80s, I ironed out the scribbles of my paper scraps, diaries, poetry, and journal writings – and composed the memoir you are about to journey through.

NOTE: For anonymity, some names and places have been changed.

This memoir is dedicated to:

Fitemi

Bentasi

Sarikki

Martina

Table of Contents

CHAPTER 1

Early Years

I closed my eyes but did not rest. He was next to me – almost invisible – until soft moonlight beaming through my jalousie steel-barred windows unveiled his visage through shadows dancing 'round his face. Those wisps of twilight skipped over his bearded chin and onto my faded bedsheets – the ones with that tiny paisley orange and blue floret print sprinkled with white daisies – brought all the way from Michigan, purchased at the Sears and Roebuck in Lansing's Frandor Plaza. My high-thread-count sheets had morphed from their smooth blueish softness into a drab gray that had become very "pilly," dulled by daily washing *avec* bar soap and stiff bristled-brushes on hand-held washboards. The reverberating of that tireless scrubbing coming from our backroom mud sink reminded me of what I was trying to forget. I stared at my old gray paper-thin sheets and realized how worn-out I had become.

It was a misty, rainy morning in Yaoundé. Listlessly preparing myself a cup of coffee, I inattentively splattered some powdered whole milk on the tiled white countertop. Wiping up the spilled powder, I sipped my *café au lait* and looked out into the parlor – for the last time – at those modish government-issued furnishings. The armchairs and sofas, all four matching and weaved with taupe-colored rattan caning, were sturdy and quite functional – although they were not all that comfortable. The caning was letting loose but still bordered by polished African teakwood in an interlocking grain pattern. They were very striking, boasting a soft chestnut tone – quite amazing for government-provided furniture. Along with the sofas and chairs, I was provided with two web-patterned teakwood end tables. I had arranged all the furnishings in a square-like design in the middle of the parlor – like an island blanketed over thousands of teal and gray ceramic mini-tiles. I studied the huge living area, spanning more than 625 square feet. It was striking and ordered and in my style – an elegant entrance to our tropical outside yard. Coffee in hand, I walked out onto the balcony and smelled the sweet fruit of mango trees. It was still raining lightly that morning when I told myself to end all my studying and looking around, shift gears, and begin thinking about what was coming next. For today was the day I was leaving. There was no other choice. Yes, I had a plan.

Waiting for Fitemi and Bentasi to wake, I crawled back into bed and drifted into a light sleep, with Sarikki cuddled between my big pregnant tummy and my pillow. My thoughts drifted back to childhood days in Iowa. I dreamed of farmland and cornfields – shadowed by my dog, Duke, cocking his head in the breeze. I remembered Dad's animated stories about 18-year-old Grandpa Klaaren traversing all kinds of obstacles to leave his Netherlands home. I was a long way from Iowa, but my memories were strong.

Rocking back and forth in that tattered old porch swing, my father's stories of Grandpa's trek to Iowa in the 1800s were amplified by Dad's very large flailing hands! Dad rambunctiously portrayed how Grandpa left his childhood home and made the arduous voyage across the vast ocean and American frontier to this country's rich, mucky soil. His destination was Iowa, a short way from Pella, a 'City of Refuge' known for its Dutch traditions. After young Ernst arrived, it wasn't long before he courted the beautiful, strong, and opinionated Hilegje Toom. Ernst and Hilegje married and settled down near the village of Eddyville. They started plowing and farming right around the turn of the century – and they also began producing their very large family. Nine children – wow! As I swung back and forth on that rickety old porch swing, I thought about how hardy folks were back then.

Mom's dad, John DeKock, came from The Netherlands too. His first wife died; years later, he met and married Jane Bauman. They ran a general store in Pella. We were told Grandpa was 30 years older than Grandma. I thought Mom's tales of the age spread were padded by the creative juices of her English skills; but Mom's life was strewn with many bouts of her dad being ill. Before Grandpa DeKock became completely bedridden, however, Grandma had three children – two boys and a girl, my mom.

Dad was the second youngest of the nine Klaaren kids. He grew up tough and rugged on a corn and wheat farm in Eddyville, Iowa. The biggest and strongest of his siblings, Dad plowed the family fields with a 4-up pack of draft horses. His parents assigned him farm work in lieu of school work. At the age of 21, Dad enrolled in the local high school academy of Central College in nearby Pella, and his parents sold their farm. During those years, the late 1920s, Marion earned his school fees shoveling coal and digging ditches. Dad was strong and steady, with big hands and a big heart. He and Cornelia DeKock became acquainted when Marion was at the Central academy while young Cornelia, two years younger than Marion, was attending Central College.

Cornelia swooned over Marion's 190-pound, muscle-built body. He was a feisty college football player – before the days of hard helmets. Cornelia was of Dutch, French, and English descent – but mostly Dutch. Mom's family also settled in Iowa – but not in the country. She was more of a "city girl," performing in high school and college operettas and singing her heart out in church on Sunday mornings. Cornelia was delicate and refined, radiating quite a sophisticated aura.

After graduating from Central College, Dad moved eastward to attend Western Theological Seminary in Holland, Michigan, where the guys called him *"Samson-strong and tough,"* and the faculty award of

"*All Around Honor*" proved he had the "stuff." Mom remained in Iowa, where she taught school in a one-room rural schoolhouse. She often described for us how she walked three miles to and from work and then started a fire – each morning. She made certain all of us kids knew that Dad's nickname for her, Kee, was based on the fact that Cornelia was the key to Marion's heart. After a long engagement, Cornelia and Marion were married in South Holland, Illinois. Uncle John, Dad's big brother, officiated at the ceremony. It was a small wedding, 'tis true, but the knot couldn't have been tied tighter.

Mom and Dad settled in the village of Conklin, Michigan, after the Great Depression had swept across the country. Dad began his first pastorship, earning a meager salary of $15 per week. Those were days when love was lived on and stretched to its very peak. Mom told me how Dad's parish members supplemented his pay with groceries, household items, and various services.

They started their family late – in those days anyway. Mom was 29, and Dad was 31 when Eugene was born; Mary Ann arrived a year later. Mom exclaimed it was like having twins – a year apart. Dad laughed when he relayed that they often made the parsonage look like a work of modern art. Keith arrived four years later. All three babes thrived while Dad was the minister at Fairview Reformed Church in Grand Rapids – from the late 30's to the mid 40's.

The Klaaren clan then moved to a small burg outside of Holland, near Lake Michigan. Dad took a different clergy position in Overisel, a tight pocket of Dutch tradition. Overisel, named after the Dutch province of *Overijssel*, was my first home. I arrived on the last day of January 1948 in the middle of a huge snowstorm. Mom's story was that while she was in hard labor, Dad stopped the Chevy to dig some stranded folks out of a snow-filled ditch.

Two days after I was born, I was named "Joy." As a teen, I wondered why it took two days to name me. But I forgot about that wonderment over the years. After Dad died, I stumbled upon a frayed book of William Blake's poems while sorting through Dad's old papers and sermons. I skimmed through the yellowed pages and noticed a checkmark next to "Infant Joy."

INFANT JOY

"I have no name;
I am but two days old.
What shall I call thee?

I happy am,
Joy is my name.
Sweet joy befall thee!

Pretty joy!
Sweet joy but two days old,
Sweet joy, I call thee;
Thou dost smile,
I sing the while,
Sweet joy befall thee!"

Wow! Was that the reason Dad named me "Joy?" Perhaps, but I'll never know for sure. I do remember the stories Mom told about how she and Dad took a lot of time deciding on my name. Being unexpected, I think I was supposed to bring "joy" to the hearts of my parents.

We moved to northwest Iowa in the 50's – Sioux Center, a farmer's paradise in great corn country, meant a very sheltered environment. Doctors made house calls and no one locked their doors. It was a quiet sanctuary, comfortably tucked away in the Bible belt.

Riding through Iowa's endless cornfields to Grandma Klaaren's place was always fun; those long family car trips were filled with counting cows, horses, and pigs – 'cause Dad instructed us to "pick a side" and keep a tally of "our" animals. He loved having us all play games while driving through Iowa's monotonous flatness: cows were 1 point, horses were 2, and pigs a negative 5. Dad engaged us to make our trips light and cheery – for it was a long ride to Grandma's. Motoring that maple-lined street and pulling up to Grandma's comfy home was a joyous time for me; as we arrived in front of her russet-bricked house, she would come running out onto the front porch, moving quite gingerly as she opened that finely-netted screen door – Grandma was already 90-something! She usually wore a floral-print long skirt, tightly fastened about her tiny waist and hanging down around her frail ankles. Her long, fine gray hair was tightly tied back in a neat bun. I remember sitting around Grandma's drop-leaf oak table with my brother, Keith, giggling as we gobbled up those freshly baked molasses cookies – and afterward scampering over to her neighbor's place to watch *"The Mickey Mouse Club Mouseketeers."*

Together, Mom and Dad beamed warmth and kindness, lovingly and creatively pooling their varied attributes. All of this trickled down, in various ways and degrees, to my three older siblings and to me. Gene, Mary Ann, Keith, and I grew up in a wonderful home. We were truly blessed.

Dad ministered to many large and devout congregations – and he and Mom were pillars in the communities we lived in. Mom and all of us assisted Dad with many church activities. In her younger years, Mom was an English and penmanship teacher – the Palmer method. Her handwriting is the most beautiful and artistic I've ever seen. She kept busy singing, teaching, and putting up with many of Dad's ideas, sometimes wacky ones!

According to my brother Keith, Dad said we could get some eggs if we raised chickens. It worked for a time, but then, one sad day, our best hen, Hennie, was stricken with some weird disease. Dad, with all his calling and praying, could not cure that poor old chick. Then Dad got an idea. With a lengthy prelude, he explained to us that he would be the surgeon and perform an operation! Mom thought it was crazy. We kids thought it was wild. But when Dad drugged that old hen to sleep, away we all ran. While Hennie was hanging by her legs, tied up on the basement water pipes, Dad began to carefully cut and remove a part or a growth or something – we weren't sure. What!?!? That chick got well again and gave us daily eggs!

Mom and Dad kept busy with the four of us. We were surrounded with love – and we thrived. So many warm childhood memories are stored inside of me:

- Raking fall leaves into tiny "leaf houses" – with Dad's hands-on supervision on how to keep the rows straight;

- Tunneling through the snow drifts, and afterward warming up with Mom's frothy homemade hot chocolate;

- Pretending to practice the "*Ballade*" and "*La Cucaracha*," music pieces in John Thompson's <u>Third Grade Book</u> – pounding down, with my little attitude, on those worn piano keys on Mom's big old spruce upright;

- Inviting over my neighborhood friends, Donna and Phyllis, to play with my coterie of eight-inch Ginger dolls;

- My friend Gladys and I devouring sticky taffy apples at Casey's Bakery on Main Street;

- Exploring our lofty, swelteringly hot attic on the top floor of the manse – accessed by that scary trap door!

- Being walked to school by my dog Duke;

- Walking hand-in-hand with my dad to visit and cheer-up senior "shut-in" parish members;

- Buying assorted roasted peanuts – in that hot glass case – at Schalekamp's Drug Store;

- Joy-riding with Keith in his '39 Hudson coupe – visiting the ice cream stands at both ends of Sioux Center;

- Asking Dad for the car and usually getting it;

- Skinny-dipping at Sandy Hollow, our local sandpit;

- Driving to Sheldon to view big-screen movies;

- Sunday after-church cruising up and down Rock Valley's downtown streets in Dad's '57 white and black Pontiac sedan – piled full with my high school buddies;

- Dad and I setting up hundreds of our tiny bricks, precisely spaced side-by-side, and then tipping over the first one and glorying in the whole set collapsing;

- Playing "Pick-Up-Sticks" with brother Gene's girlfriend, Mary;

- My big sister Mary Ann treating me to a drive-in movie in Hawarden and exiting with the theater's speaker still attached to our rear car window;

- Tagging along with Dad, Gene, and his college frat brothers to hunt pheasants and jack rabbits in those snowy Iowa cornfields;

- Our tent collapsing in the middle of the night;

- Dad and I strolling through the snow to Boeyink's Grocery store to pick out the best-shaped Christmas tree.

My childhood was content. I did all the happy, wholesome things.

When Mom and Dad celebrated their 25th wedding anniversary, I was in junior high school and the only child living at home. Eugene was attending graduate school at Harvard, Mary Ann was teaching high school English in Hawaii, and Keith was enrolled at Hope College. My three siblings posted family remembrances to that big anniversary gathering in our church's basement. Those letters, which revealed a lot about our life as a family, were shared with the entire congregation at that celebration.

Gene's letter, entitled "Oatmeal Time," stretched the truth a bit but humorously illustrated our family meal times together.

"If one asks what occurrence in the life of the Klaaren family is unique or what occurrence best portrays the flavor of our family life, I MUST answer (with some hesitation) that it is oatmeal.

Oatmeal was not only food in our family life; it was an ordeal. Does this sound strange or odd? Well, it should – let me explain!

Oatmeal played a major role in our family when we were together. Oatmeal was served as breakfast in our home every day, seven days a week, 52 weeks per year, year after year. Whether anyone **wanted** oatmeal, **needed** oatmeal, or **liked** oatmeal – this just did not make any difference. Regardless of tastes, needs, or consequences, everyone (including VISITORS) ate oatmeal for breakfast at our house. Why oatmeal? Simply because Dad said so, and that was it. Now let me describe a typical morning at our house and the role of oatmeal. But please, don't let the foul flavor of oatmeal preoccupy your attention. It is the family life I'm trying to illustrate.

Almost every morning before breakfast, while Mary Ann, Keith, Joy, and I were upstairs waiting for the fateful morning call, the argument would begin. We would listen to Mom and Dad arguing down in the kitchen. The argument was always (day in and day out) about oatmeal. You see, Mom didn't really go for oatmeal, and thus, in order to make sure we would all be treated to oatmeal, Dad would always have to tromp downstairs early in the morning and cook it himself.

When all of us were assembled 'round the table, the oatmeal was brought forth, and the usual reactions would begin. Great agony and ordeal characterized the occasion. Now, in the first place, Mom always managed to be very quiet, and thus, when the dreadful pot of oatmeal came circling around the table (in Dad's steady hands), Dad was very merciful and gave her only a little. Boy, was she lucky!

Mary Ann was always the second victim. She would always scream and holler bloody murder, 'not oatmeal again!' However, this never made any difference. Dad always stopped her howls with the deadly **Plop-Plop-Plop** of lumpy oatmeal splashing in her bowl. If just the sound of oatmeal didn't do the trick, then he would feed her – and this always worked.

Keith and I were served next. We never cried or screamed. You see, for us, oatmeal was a matter of competition and conditioning. This was the way we asserted our manhood. Not that we liked the stuff, indeed nobody in their right mind does, but, for Keith and me, it was a contest to see who could eat the most. We never could out-eat Dad! We were so conditioned to the stuff that we actually began to think it was pretty good. What a dream. I'm on cream of wheat now, and I'll never eat oatmeal again.

The last person to be served every morning was little Joy. Poor girl, she didn't cry often, but defenseless as she was, she also was fed oatmeal. There used to be a rumor in our family that Joy was actually weaned on oatmeal, but I think that would be stretching it a bit.

Now, I must say that somewhat more seriously, I have exaggerated in places. Really, these big breakfasts together did much for us as a family. Dad was often gone to meetings, committees, calling, etc., in the evenings and we never then had much time to get together as a family. Thus, our mornings (in spite of oatmeal) have really been formative influences in our lives. Love, Gene"

Eugene's story showed humorous – yet warm and loving -- glimpses of our family life. Another participant in the celebration was my sister, Mary Ann, the poet:

"I know you're 'pastor and wife' here – I'm a 'Preacher's Kid' cuz of you,
And Central Church has called me to reveal WHAT PREACHERS DO!

This is quite an assignment -- Could be quite a plight
Perhaps it is a good thing that I'm really out of sight.

But – please don't worry – you know I don't know much;
For when I was so little

You spoke such things in Dutch!"

I can remember Mom's story of when Dad, just once, preached a sermon in Dutch. Mom said that Dad's Dutch skills were pretty poor. She encouraged Dad to stick with English.

My brother, Keith, also shared a letter with great flashbacks to growing up in the 50's:

- "Remember my dump truck, the one that had to have its burrs loosened and tightened daily?

- How Mary Ann used to scream when Mom put those rag curlers in her hair;

- When T.V. invaded our town and everyone thought it was fascinating but, of course we didn't get it because there were better things to spend our money on than such nonsense;

- I somehow got the impression that anyone who didn't vote would go to Hell for sure;

- The time I thought I saved the church from being burned down when I picked up that cigarette a parishioner threw in the grass, and I began to puff on it – right when Dad came around the corner – and I thought I'd really accomplished something; instead Dad said nothing and he took me straight home and put me in my room and gave me one of those wedding cigars; I puffed on it and after while I didn't feel so good; I got the idea Dad didn't want me to smoke;

- Great times playing ping pong on the table you built, Dad;

- Then there was Uncle John who would try to sell you on those wonderful Kaiser Frazer products – but you said our '36 Plymouth was a good car, and it would have to do;

- Our stay in the little white cottage with red trim on big Lake Michigan; we were crowded, but we had fun;

- Stopping for ice cream cones at the Milk Bottle Dairy in Joliet;

- The struggle between the two powers, my sister Mary Ann and Dad, over the principles of geometry; Mary Ann was positive the principles had changed since Dad's academy days;

- The "Battle for the Rat" in the Sioux Center parsonage with our Eskimo Spitz Duke of Klaarensville; we had a visitor one night; we heard it inside the walls gnaw and claw; Mom said it was a monstrous rat; Dad said it was just a wee church mouse who came to our house to feel safe; it was evident Mom was right; so Dad tried to catch him with wire traps set with cheese; but alas it was Duke who captured the fat rat – which admitted 'The Duke' to the Klaaren family;

- Thank you, Mom and Dad, for explaining that situations are not always black or white, but sometimes can be a bit blurred; it's not always a question of what is right or wrong but usually what is wise or unwise;

- Thanks for allowing me to do things and go places – and to hitch-hike;

- Thanks for guiding me in decisions, but yet actually allowing me to make them and helping me in carrying them out;

- Thanks for having faith in me, not a blind faith, but one that is constantly fluctuating;

- I thank you, Mother and Dad, for the food, clothing, shelter, and love that you have always provided;

- May the next 25 years be as happy as the first 25.

- With love, Keith Alan Klaaren"

My siblings and I had a wholesome upbringing. I was raised in a loving and devoted family, growing up as the youngest daughter of a schoolteacher and a preacher. I was lucky to be a part of a loving two-parent family. It certainly isn't the fortuitous fate of everyone.

But subtly wrapped around this caring and loving was the baggage carried with my parents from their own struggles, experiences, and traditions. Life is rarely tidy. My mom had suffered from severe depression. I remember her leaving for a short time. Where did she go?

Times were tough for a while, yet Dad was always her strength and support. He truly loved her, which was apparent to me and my sister and brothers – but there were just some things that never were talked about.

Then there were the congregation members who wished Dad to preach and conduct the parish a certain way. I don't remember all the scenarios, for I was not yet grown, but it seemed to me that my father was banging his head up against a brick wall in many instances. How could this be? Dad was the most tolerant, understanding, loving person I had ever known. Strangers would come to him when no one else would listen or help them.

A strong picture in my mind was when a young, shabbily dressed girl arrived at our house on Main Street. She knocked on our front porch screen door early that morning. I remember because Mom sent me to answer the door. She seemed to be around my age, and tears were running down her gaunt cheeks. "Is this the preacher's place?" she pleaded. I told her that, indeed, my father was a minister, and I asked her to wait while I went to find him. I hurried up to Dad's study to tell him about the morning visitor and how forlorn and shabby she looked. Dad went to the door and invited her into our home. He spent many hours with that little child. He told me later that her name was Wilhemina and that she had nowhere to go. My father made sure Wilhemina was taken care of.

Dad showed me daily that he was a servant and a disciple. He always spent more time with people than with programs, committees, meetings, and all that other church stuff. Many of our community folks didn't think the same way Dad thought. He was my hero.

Here's a lesson I learned from my father. Occasionally, I would question Dad about religion, probably because he was a preacher.

"Hey, Dad, I don't see how praying can help anyone," I muttered.

I can still see him sprawled out across that tattered old wood swing hung up high on our screened-in porch.

"Joy, it's important to know how to pray and what to pray for. Praying isn't just asking for things. You know that your friend, Wayne, is handicapped, right? And that Wayne's father, Jim, has emphysema, which will cut short his life if he doesn't stop smoking? Well, Joy, the family is very poor, and they have prayed a lot. I counseled Jim about prayer, and he finally got the idea. I want to share with you a lesson about prayer. Here are Jim's words."

"When I asked God to take away my bad smoking habit, God said: **NO. It isn't for me to take away, but for you to give up.** When I asked God to make my handicapped child whole, God said: **NO. His spirit is whole; his body is only temporary.** When I asked God to give me happiness, God said: **NO. I give you all kinds of blessings. Happiness is up to you.** When I asked God for all the things that I needed to enjoy life, God said: **NO. I will give you life so that you may enjoy all things.** When I asked God to help me love others as much as He loves me, God said: **Ahhhh – Finally, you have the idea.**"

Dad taught me lots of important stuff. Growing up in the 1950s in a small northwestern Iowa town, I had a happy childhood. I lived, played, attended school, and interacted with predominately folks of Dutch descent – just like me. My home town was the perfect place to grow up – in most ways. My world was made up of family activities, school friends, and countless church endeavors. All of this was because I was grounded by a loving and caring family. Exploring my town was always an adventure. Duke and I often walked the sidewalks of Sioux Center. The hardware store was filled with tools and items I had never heard of – all kinds of stuff Dad and I collected to put together a mini working water-pump for my junior high science project, the best in the class! Yeah! Schalekamp's Drug Store had those hot roasted peanuts. The town bakery was my favorite – and Duke, my Eskimo Spitz, liked their sweets too.

There was little diversity in my town, however, and my contact with folks different from me was rare – except when I traveled with Dad to Nebraska, where he conducted prayer meetings at a Sioux Native

American church. I loved going with Dad on those trips; usually, he asked me to play the piano for the hymn singing. But one time, when there was no piano available, I wandered around the reservation socializing with the young Sioux adolescents who had become my friends. On one occasion, I was invited to smoke a peace pipe. My friends had filled the pipe with peyote! When Dad found me giggling with my friends, he was not pleased! I told Dad that the pipe was used for a religious purpose; however, my story was not received well.

Maybe, on account of my father's desire to leave the family farm as a young man, I, too, wanted to venture outside of that little town in Iowa. Or maybe I wanted to mimic my older siblings who had left to see the world. I wanted to experience more of life, and I felt the community I lived in was holding me back. I craved learning about art, literature, science – everything. I believed I was ready to go away to college. Perhaps I was more concerned with what my parents were not able to provide for me instead of the many blessings they provided.

As I matured, I grew to understand the limitations of those who loved me – and love them for the countless bounties they provided. Mom and Dad always had time for me and for all my siblings. And even more vital than time, I was taught by my parents to love and respect people – all people.

In the mid-60s, when Dad was nearing retirement age, he accepted a new position near Battle Creek, Michigan – a position in a church with a smaller congregation than the one in Iowa. For me, it was an opportunity to leave Iowa and see the world!

However, because I was a senior class officer and the editor of my high school yearbook, I dutifully remained in Sioux Center to honor my commitments. Mom and Dad allowed me the choice to accompany them or to stay with some family friends. I chose to remain in Iowa – but only temporarily.

My thoughts were filled with the anticipation of going to Michigan, making new friends there, and seeing my parent's new home. After I completed the first semester at Sioux Center High, I joined Dad and Mom to complete my final semester of high school in Michigan. I looked forward to attending Hope College the following year.

CHAPTER 2

College Years

My first year of college began with enthusiasm. Dad drove Mom and me to the corner of 10th and Columbia, and we all jumped out and transported my stuff up to the 2nd floor of Phelps Hall; I had become a college freshman in the mid-60's! I was very excited to meet my two roommates, explore the campus "Pine Grove," and to swankily fix-up Room 204 in Phelps Hall – in a combo of our very own styles. That semester was full of many fresh happenings. It was pretty easy to adapt to life away from home.

As the year continued on into the second semester, I began to dwell on how things in college were different than in my small town in Iowa or even in the school I attended in Springfield. Back in high school, I was involved in many activities, both academically and socially. But I knew nothing about what was going on in the rest of the country or in the larger world.

Now, it seemed like there were so many big issues. In the Phelps Hall lounge, I watched clips and snippets on TV of the free speech movement, the Vietnam War, racial injustice, and the diminished position of women.

There were protests and demonstrations at the University of Michigan and in California at Berkeley. I wondered about all the political events and many other issues. Most of my peers didn't seem to think those things mattered all that much. They were more concerned with who would take them to see "*Alfie*" or "*Who's Afraid of Virginia Wolf*" at the Holland or Park Theatre. The dating and social scenes were important to many students; and I kind of wanted to be involved in those things too, but unconsciously, I realized that I would need to shed some pounds in order to be "out there" with those other girls. So, I concentrated on being informed and learning about new perspectives, which I thought was a smart direction -- and I joined the International Relations Club. It was a great outlet for me, for I met interesting students from many countries around the world. I began to concentrate on doing well in school – to enable a promising career. Studying occupied practically all of my time – except when I helped friends and acquaintances with their homework. There was not much support academically for students who were struggling, and studying was not the common pattern for many young coeds. Many evenings and week-ends, I sat sprawled out on the stairways of Lubbers Hall, tutoring classmates taking Dr. Brady's introduction to biology class. Although I had friends, many of my classmates looked at me as the "brainy one." I didn't always like that perception they had of me. I wanted to be more than the smart one; but I didn't know what it was I wanted. Perhaps I was just having the usual mundane experience of a young, inexperienced girl starting life.

When Spring Break appeared, I planned an excursion to the Chicago Institute of Art, hoping it would lift my spirits. Few of my friends enjoyed my love of art, so I failed to interest my roommates or anyone else to accompany me. Little did I know that walking out of my dorm room and down the street to the Greyhound bus station would turn out to be a tragic move. It was nearing the end of my first year in college when I innocently walked into an awful ordeal that I failed to reveal for decades – and am now relaying for the first time.

Arriving in Chicago on a very busy afternoon, I curiously and anxiously stepped out of the Greyhound bus station and walked into the city's bustling activity. Leaving Union Station and strolling Chicago's sidewalks was amazing. Seeing hundreds of faces – all kinds of people – was something new and exciting for me. As a child raised in that small Iowa town, I felt all the Chicago folks were friendly and trustworthy. I was thirsty and walked into a diner for a soda.

A friendly young man approached and sat down next to me. In my naïve fashion, I struck up a conversation. We chatted for a while, and when he asked me to go for a walk, I agreed! He said his name was Bill. While walking down the street, he told me he wanted to stop at his place to pick up something very important. When I walked up the steps, he pushed me inside and locked the door! OMG! What was wrong with me? Why was I so trusting and senseless? Unlike many memories, this one is clear and will not go away. It's sharply embedded in me. How could I have been so unsuspecting?

The poorly lit room was filthy and smelly. He pushed me onto the couch.

"Lay down, bitch," he shouted.

"No," I yelled.

Forcing me towards him, he ripped off my blouse and yanked my bra up around my neck, grabbing my breasts! When I felt his fingers squeezing my throat, I pulled myself loose and attempted to crawl away. But he jumped me and violently threw me onto his bed. From the foot-end, he thrust himself into me over and over again without my permission. The pain was unimaginable. I can't find words to describe my agony.

I must have passed out, for when I opened my eyes, he was gone. I didn't know where, but I prayed he would not return. Sharp pains shot through my body as I pulled myself up. I was sore and bruised from wrestling and resisting his attack. Blood dribbled down the inside of both my legs. I knew I had to run – before he returned. I don't know how I had the strength, but I ran for many blocks looking for a taxi. Finally flagging one down, the driver took me to the bus station. I bought a ticket back to Holland.

Back on Hope College's campus, I felt I didn't know who I was anymore. I felt dead. I wanted to be invisible. I wanted to be silent and never speak of it. Why hadn't he just killed me? I was damaged and violated – invaded without my consent. Even though my background taught me that everyone was my friend, I had learned that it was not true.

I cried for days, not wanting to go out of my dormitory room. I don't recollect much about the weeks following the rape. I do remember that I became withdrawn. I recall many periods of despair. I hid under my bed for two days! When one of my dorm sisters found me, the resident advisor arranged for me to talk to a campus psychologist. Those counseling sessions touched only the surface. Guilt for taking a walk with a total stranger encompassed my life. Anger boiled over in me, but I repressed it. I could not bring myself to tell anyone about that horrific incident! I was silent.

Food became my best friend. My newly acquired svelte body began to slowly vanish. I gained lots of weight. I thought that if I looked unattractive, no one would want to touch me. Near the end of the term, I swallowed an entire bottle of aspirins! I have a vague memory of the emergency room and my ringing ears. Arrangements were made to postpone my final exams. I longed for summer. I wished I could return to the gentler times in small-town Sioux Center, where Duke and I would run to the town bakery or to Boeyink's Grocery – where I would be enjoying a simpler, safer life.

I was ashamed of my stupidity. I thought how vulnerable a little lamb would be when attacked by a mountain lion. But that lamb would not have walked right into the lion's den!

Was it my fault? In some ways, my inner feelings were how I imagined Hester Prynne would have felt in Nathaniel Hawthorne's The Scarlett Letter – being judged and identified as a sinner.

Nineteen (by Joy Klaaren)

Sharing all my body's secrets was for me,
at age nineteen,
Built on wonders only dreamed of –
I was young and filled with life.
Imagination lived inside me.
The world I held in my young hands.
Long ago, I was enchanted by fresh thoughts of love – so grand.
I was growing – girl to woman – jeans to dresses,
buttons and bows
--Laughing, playing, ripe with wonder
-- blooming like morn's first red rose.

But never, never in my dreaming
Did I ever quite foresee
How that callous, "soul-less" man
Would take my dreams away from me

I wandered through my formative years without telling my story to anyone. Having grown up in a quiet, isolated, and homogenous environment, it was hard for me to believe what had just happened. If only I had not gone on that walk with a complete stranger and had not willingly entered his apartment – maybe then I could have asked someone for help. After the rape, I was very hesitant to involve the police. I was ashamed that I had been so stupid. Why didn't I know better? That failure to share led me on a path where I saw myself as responsible – instead of seeing myself as a victim. I was consumed by my guilt. I believe that my Chicago trauma and my following depression and dispiritedness shaped, in many unfortunate ways, the rest of my life.

Managing to carry on and stay in college for a while, I delved into my courses. During my sophomore year, I was enrolled in an art history class. I remember that particular class because of a certain student who was always watching me. My first look at him was in that class, and I wondered why he didn't belong to the international club. After class, he walked up to me, and we introduced ourselves. He said his name was Christopher, and he came from Cameroon. Wow! I had never met anyone from Cameroon before. I was intrigued. In my mind, I thought that his trans-Atlantic journey from Cameroon made my journey from Iowa seem insignificant.

Christopher did not call or contact me, and we had no more classes together after Dr. Benesch's Art History course. I was very disappointed because I was curious about his background and his Cameroonian culture -- and I was also curious about him, wanting to know more about him. He sparked something in me for many reasons, but I didn't recognize all of them. I told myself that my interest in him was because I had never had a close friendship with anyone from any other place other than in Iowa or Michigan. But a further connection between us did not happen. I continued to carry out my school responsibilities. My mind was heavy with many emotions – or, to be more correct, many unexpressed emotions – the silence. I continued to sign in and to see the Hope College psychologist. Nothing was helping me, so when I left for home at the end of the term, I was pretty certain I would not be returning to Hope College. During the following summer, I worked at the local Heinz Pickle factory in Holland, Michigan. It was a miserable job; the odor of vinegar severely invaded my clothes, hair, and skin.

After earning enough money to travel, I planned on heading to California. It was a sunny and far-away place where I thought I would try to "find myself" – whatever that meant. My family reluctantly supported my planned excursion because they had some – but very little – understanding of my turmoil. They were confused about what was bothering me, and so was I. Was I making a wise decision? Why did I leave Hope College? Was it going to be helpful to take a little vacation away from home with my sister and her husband? I thought it was a perfect scenario for me. My brother-in-law, Ken, was a professor of communication at the University of Michigan. He was taking his sabbatical, serving as a visiting professor at the University of Southern California – in Los Angeles. I hoped that he and my big sis would be happy to accommodate me. In my mind, I had to go somewhere to escape my thoughts about Chicago. Mom and Dad had little idea about what was going on in my mind. They probably thought that Mary Ann and Ken could help me, being that they were both communication professors. But I didn't want to break my silence; I certainly did not want to talk about it. Lucky for me they all agreed with my plan. Mary Ann and Ken sent me a long letter in anticipation of my arrival in Los Angeles.

"February 7, 1968

Dear Joy,

We feel somewhat unsure of what we should say in this letter to you. In large part this is due to our lack of knowledge as to the situation in which you find yourself. Before we call you at one o'clock your time on Sunday, we're hoping to have received the letter from your therapist, giving us more insight concerning your situation, etc. . . . ."

The neatly typed letter continued on for nearly three pages, written in my sister and brother-in-law's professional style -- outlining in great detail what my responsibilities would be during my stay with them. I appreciated their kindness and concern, but I didn't want rules, responsibilities and duties; I was looking for a way to understand the rape I had endured in Chicago. Not finding what I wanted, I embraced an imprudent lifestyle. California was a new world for me – similar to the excitement of the young girl Dorothy in the old classic movie when she realized she was no longer in Kansas. I gazed at the evening colorful lighting shining on all the apartments in the hills overlooking USC. It was stunning and exciting. Nothing in LA was conventional, like what I was accustomed to in Iowa.

I began running around with an incorrigible crowd. My new-found friends were not bad people, just free spirits. I wanted to be an activist flower-child of the 60's. Mary Ann and Ken suspected a weird streak in me when I moved out of their apartment. I looked for employment and was hired at a lending/credit loan business near Crenshaw Blvd., Universal CIT. With money coming in I was able to contribute needed funds to my friends at their apartment. Partying and senselessness abounded. We spent our evenings carousing and our days swimming in the complex's pool. My sister and her husband were baffled by my atypical behavior and activities. Mary Ann and Ken must have wondered what happened to the sweet, wholesome young lady they thought they knew.

Then, a phone call came from my college friend in Michigan. She told me that my former roommate had been assaulted and raped on 10th Street – and the college was attempting to keep it quiet and out of the newspapers! Oh no! She was abducted walking home from an evening class. Memories of my own horrific Chicago ordeal came back to rattle and shake my senses. I felt deeply for my friend – but I was not willing to share my vicious attack and rape! My experience was private – known only to me – and it would remain private for another time.

I became disoriented and needed to confide in someone. I booked a flight back to Mom and Dad's place in Michigan. Hiding in my old bedroom on Goguac Street, I cried for hours, trying to come up with the courage to talk to my parents – but I just couldn't! I avoided participating in any family activities. Home for barely one week, I just wanted to retreat to a place no one knew me or about me. I could only think returning to California would be ideal. California, here I come!

On that warm June evening, my parents went next door for their weekly Sunday night church service, where my father would be preaching. As I listened for the congregation to sing the first hymn, I telephoned for a cab. Scurrying around my room, I picked up a few items and tossed them into my suitcase. The taxi arrived. I rode down to the Battle Creek bus station and boarded a Greyhound bound for Chicago. I was intending to fly back to California. When I arrived at O'Hare, I changed my mind. Within hours, I was on my way to the home of my brother, Gene, and his wife, Mary. Needless to mention, they were shocked to find me on their doorstep. We talked and laughed for a little while, but I did not address the issues that played in my mind. I wanted to share, but I could not do it; I left Connecticut and continued my journey back to Los Angeles.

The flight to Cali was routed through O'Hare in Chicago. While I waited in the airport to change planes, a flight attendant delivered a message to me that I had an emergency telephone call in the terminal. Supposing that it was my dad, I was startled to hear my therapist's voice on the phone. He did all he could to persuade me to return home. But I listened to no one. I know I possess a stubborn streak.

Arriving in "sunny California," I felt a sense of possible renewal in the land of opportunity. I hung out in the "City of Angels" for close to two weeks. Where was I going to stay? I answered a couple of advertisements in *The Los Angeles Times* and found a tiny room in a pretty sleazy neighborhood near Echo Park. It wasn't long before I started making bad choices – but to be truthful, I can't remember all the choices I made, but I do remember that they were not good ones. As I was running out of alternatives, survival won out, perhaps because my money started to run out. My enjoyment of the irresponsible lifestyle I had somewhat enjoyed and luckily weathered weeks earlier was subsiding. It was not easy for me to admit making poor decisions, but eventually, I came to much better options. Perhaps I was not able to forsake my ancestors' industriousness, academic prowess, and kindness – maybe some *"dribblings"* of those traits were part of my own DNA.

The money dried up, and the fun ended. With the last of my dollars dwindling, I said my goodbyes to my friends and acquaintances in California. The "prodigal daughter" returned home. I inconsiderately did not inform my parents of my return until I arrived at the train depot on Burdick Street in Kalamazoo. I was astonished how quickly Dad arrived at the station – I thought he must have, uncharacteristically, broke the speed limit! Mom and Dad enveloped me with unconditional hugs and expressions of love – and those affections were quite welcomed and remarkable, given that we were not a very "touchy/feely" family. My parents felt relief when they saw me. But Gene, Mary Ann and Keith exhibited a more punitive stance. "Punish her for causing so much trouble" was my siblings' solution to my escapades. Little did I know Dad had hired a private detective to locate me in California.

Quite remarkably, and perhaps manipulatively, I persuaded Mom and Dad to arrange another trip for me – to spend the rest of the summer with my cousin, John DeKock, in Ramona, California. My parents sensed that I was struggling, so they made a familial excursion possible – to Mom's nephew's place located about forty miles northeast of San Diego. John was a physician in quite a sparsely populated desert area. His practice was located in the town of Ramona, but he and his family lived on a cattle ranch. Ranch living sounded like another great adventure. I rarely ever rode a horse, and the thought of bouncing in a saddle seemed exhilarating. I was searching for some sense of happiness and well- being. His ranch had so many amenities, including a swimming pool, a sauna, and, of course, horses. I enjoyed myself for a while – until despair set in. I had too much time to think. What stands out in my mind was being alone in their quaint guesthouse alongside the pool. I thought about talking with my cousin; after all, he was a medical doctor. I wondered if he would understand. But I was still consumed by my own accountability for what had happened in Chicago. My grief was too severe, and I popped an overdose of aspirin. Cousin John found me, treated me, and saw to it I recovered – physically. Emotionally, I was a wreck. Of course, he contacted my parents. Shortly after my father arrived in California, he took me by the hand and back home to Michigan, and I was admitted into Pine Rest Christian Hospital, fifty miles from my parent's home in Springfield.

My hospital reprieve was short and unproductive, for the most part. I didn't want to be there, and I did little to help myself. My therapist, whose name I've forgotten, was a compassionate man. But I don't remember much about our sessions. Hours and days of counseling extended to weeks and weeks of more counseling; I attended all the sessions, but I was more driven by the thought of leaving than by the prospect of healing and getting better. I just didn't want to talk – to anyone. I was not willing to discuss my previous life and issues. If I was going to communicate about my rape, it was going to have to be with a trusted, loving friend. I learned to do and say the things and words needed to be discharged from the hospital, and I accomplished that – all the little things that gave the illusion that I had recovered.

Margie and Sue were also patients in that hospital; the three of us became great friends during our residence there. When I was discharged, Sue and Margie were set to leave the next week, and the three of us decided to live together. Sue and I looked for employment opportunities. Grand Rapids Public Library hired me as a front desk check-out clerk. The work was pleasant, but the library job was boring and definitely not challenging. As for my two roommates, Sue found a job quickly, and Margie was supported by her parents, so she didn't need to work. The three of us were thrilled to find an apartment on the second floor of a dated old house on Fairview Street off of Coit. Even though that dilapidated two-story rental was in ill-repair, it was positioned on the top of a high hill overlooking the city. The view astonished all of us. It was breathtaking. From the bay window ledge, we could see the entire metropolitan area. In the evenings, there was a soft glow from neon signs and streetlights. Those were good times with good friends, but for me, there were issues still hidden beneath the surface.

My desire to return to college was clouded by a distressing recollection. I kept on working for what I wasn't sure. When our landlord sold the Fairview house, we had to move. We located another apartment quickly. The new place was a second-floor bungalow off Fulton Street – near downtown Grand Rapids. The street, Portsmouth, was so narrow it looked like an alley. We loved the location on that quaint tiny one-way alley, and we liked the apartment a lot – particularly because of the antique claw-foot bathtub. All three of us worked on our respective issues as best we could.

As for myself, I tried to bury myself in my job and forget about those never-ending plans to return to school. I remained bored with my job at the library, however, so I looked for other employment. It wasn't long before I was working at a downtown department store, Herpolsheimer's, in the toy department, which had an annoying tiny train putt-putting around on a track above the merchandise. That job, too, was interesting for only a very short time. I continued to be drawn, reluctantly, to return to college – with the hope of developing some kind of promising career. I decided to try a new approach – a different place. I applied for admission to the University of Michigan. I was anxious to continue my education, but going back to Hope College was not something I thought I could handle. I wanted a fresh start. When my letter of acceptance into Michigan arrived, things started to look better. Attending the U of M thrilled me!

One sunny weekend in the middle of May, Sue and I drove to Holland to visit Sue's parents – and to attend the annual Tulip Time Festival. However, the coed radar drew us to a Hope College party. As we walked around the corner of Central Avenue and 13th, we heard the music of Sly and the Family Stone's *"Everyday People."* We continued on to a shabby off-campus house where we saw students bustling in and out, and we heard music playing. As we approached, I could see that both floors were packed with college students. Entering through the front door, the smell of smoke and beer permeated the air.

I recognized a certain young man conversing on the other side of the room. He was Christopher Forgwe, the young Cameroonian who I met in my art history class the year before. I motioned to him, and he came over to the doorway where Sue and I were standing. We talked and laughed, attempting to get reacquainted 'midst all the party noise and commotion.

When a new song, *"Son of a Preacher Man,"* began, Christopher asked me to dance. I enjoyed the dance, and he seemed to enjoy it too.

He asked if I liked the music of Dusty Springfield. I said I didn't know who Dusty Springfield was. Christopher laughed, and then he asked me why I left Hope College. I made up some excuse. That was not the time to get personal.

Before returning to Grand Rapids on Saturday, Sue and I attended some of the Tulip Time festivities, where we watched the colorful Klompen Dancers in Centennial Park and viewed the festive parade of marching bands. But my thoughts were neither on the dancers nor the bands, for all I could think about were the plans I made at the college party the night before – with a certain young man. Christopher and I had arranged a breakfast rendezvous for the following weekend.

The Windmill Restaurant became a favorite spot for Christopher and I to enjoy bran muffins, coffee, and conversation. We met there often. Soon we graduated to listening to records and getting better acquainted in Christopher's Meyer Cottage room on Columbia Avenue – the campus cottage where he resided. We agreed to continue seeing each other.

I informed my roommates, Sue and Margie, that I would be terminating my job and moving to my parent's home in Springfield, near Battle Creek. Staying with my mom and dad, I regularly used Dad's car to drive to Holland and visit Christopher. One thing led to another, and I re-entered Hope College. My University of Michigan plans were forgotten.

CHAPTER 3

Best Friends, Marriage, and Disenchantment

My impression of Christopher Forgwe was that he was clean-cut, intelligent, and intriguing. He looked to be about six feet tall, and he had a stocky, muscular build. His hair was starting to vanish, however, and he nursed a slight limp – but it was impossible to resist his engaging smile. Christopher's buoyant spirit captivated everyone around him. And his voice! It was incredibly charming, with a touch of an English accent. This guy was definitely not from Kansas, much less from Iowa. He appeared to be curious, open, adventuresome, and quite enterprising. As we shared our backgrounds, my vicious ordeal in Chicago was not mentioned. Besides, what local adventurous exploits could I offer? My life had been family, church, and friends. Chris shared a few things about his life – that he worked for five years in the Bamenda court system, that his mother worked her own ground-nut farm in their home village of Njindom where there was no electricity or running water, and that he was twenty-four years old. Well,

I reasoned that I, too, must be wise and interesting; beyond everything, I was able to hold his attention.

Days became months; our relationship developed and grew stronger. Those were memorable times. Christopher was a great conversationalist. While absorbed in class discussions and debates, other students admired him, and at parties and social functions, folks gathered around him. Vicariously, I, too, felt important and welcomed; after all, I was his companion.

Chris and I became inseparable. I admired his intelligence and creativity, and he cherished my friendly and bubbly personality. We talked and laughed together, we read together, we cooked together, we ate together, we went on day road-trips together, we played Scrabble together, we danced together. We rustled through the crisp autumn leaves. Autumn came and went, and winter arrived. We played in the snow, slipping icy snowballs down each other's backs. We took long hikes. We packed picnic lunches. We strolled along the beach at Tunnel Park in the cold. We intimately shared our private selves, releasing feelings and unveiling senses we never knew existed. We discussed philosophers such as Bonhoeffer, Sartre, Aristotle, and Russell. We reflected on the works of classic artists – Monet, Dali, Rembrandt, Renoir. We enjoyed Beethoven's symphonies – all nine of them. We listened to J. S. Bach. Chris helped me with my English essays for that ENG 232 class. I performed, for him, Handel's *Trumpet Voluntary* on that old beat-up piano in Nykerk Hall. We listened to Mozart while quaffing a few too many. Vivaldi soothed our personal concerns.

Christoper and I became best friends and lovers. But what about that horrific trauma I had experienced in Chicago the year before? Should I tell Christopher all about it now? Was he the friend I could trust with my trauma? Would he understand and be supportive and help me endure it? My silence haunted me, so I tucked it away really deep inside of me, hiding it away from my friends and my family. Thinking that my new-found friend and lover would understand and help me bear my trauma, I decided to tell him my story.

It was late, and our class assignments were completed. We were sprawled out on the oak floor of Christopher's Meyer Cottage room, sorting through some assorted LP record albums. I had a difficult time getting started, but I managed to come up with the words.

Quite reluctantly, I muttered: "Christopher, there's something I really want to share with you. Last spring-break, I took a Greyhound bus to Chicago to enjoy some art. When I got off the bus, the number of people coming and going was totally amazing. I stopped at a diner for a Coke -- and a friendly young man sat down right next to me. We started talking, and before I knew it, he asked me to go with him on a walk. He seemed very nice, so I walked down the sidewalk with …."

Christopher jumped up off the floor and started yelling at me, "Why would you be so fucking stupid as to take a walk with a stranger – a total stranger?"

"I don't know. I don't know," I whimpered.

I stopped talking. I said nothing more. I never got my story out – to him or to me!

Chris turned away. Sensing his annoyance and anger, I began trembling and crying. Christopher said nothing more. He asked no more questions. And I didn't volunteer to reveal any more about the situation. He left his room, and I went back to mine. We never talked about it again.

Everything changed. We didn't talk for days. Chris accused me of many things – with no basis. Christopher became a stranger to me. And he certainly didn't understand my trauma. He didn't know me at all, and I became skeptical of his character. Our relationship was suffering and slipping away, but somehow, ironically, we continued to visit each other – occasionally. Those times were tumultuous and full of accusations. I accused him of not being understanding of my turmoil. He accused me of being stupid and making unwise choices. I said he lacked understanding and tolerance. He said I never felt anything for him because I was sneaking around and seeing someone else. I explained that Victor was one of my good friends. He didn't care. Chris blew everything out of proportion. Victor and I were classmates and friends who talked and laughed a lot – but what was wrong with a platonic relationship like that? We were not "dating." Christopher flew off the handle. He attacked me, striking my back over and over again. I was pinned between the bed and the wall – squeezed tightly and unable to move; but Chris continued hitting me and hitting me until there was blood dripping down my arm! Suddenly, he stopped and backed away. Wounded, I ran to my safe house on 9th Street. Lying on the cool hardwood floors, I gazed at the ceiling, overcome with tears.

I attempted to end everything with Christopher. From my apartment, I discarded every reminder of him – from the pics we took of each other on that sandy little mini-beach in Douglas to the slides of us behind those trees overlooking Tunnel Park. Then I stormed over to Meyer Cottage and collected my records, clothing, shoes, photos, and all "Chris & Joy" mementos from his room. A few weeks passed, and Chris implored me to "return to him."

What!?! I didn't understand. He must love me, I thought. Perhaps so, but the aggression was overwhelming. Was there a reason for it? I didn't think a reunion would be wise.

I filled my time renewing old comforting friendships with some dormitory comrades and roommates. Christopher walked over to my cave often to let me know he felt I was ignoring him. One morning, after I had just returned home from my Heinz Pickle night job, Christopher knocked on my front door on 9th Street. As I slowly yet cautiously opened it and peeked out, he lunged at me, striking my face – and then he attempted to hug me!!! What was going on? I could sense that he was full of emotion. Were these unusual sentiments built on jealousy, on grief, or what? Both of us were pretty overwhelmed. Yet I, as always – being the dutiful companion – attempted to re-ignite our rapport. Christopher declared he had missed me.

I knew reuniting was not wise, so I planned a brief "think-it-over" time with my brother, Gene, and his family. The day before I left for my brother's house, I let Christopher know that I thought our relationship was still in trouble -- that it wasn't working very well. When I arrived in Middletown, my family connection there was just what I needed. They welcomed me, and we conversed while taking some scenic rides through the New England countryside. They tried to advise me.

While in Connecticut, Chris called me to apologize for every cruel thing he ever said or did to me. He was crying uncontrollably on the phone.

"I love you, Joy," were the words that came out of Christopher's mouth.

"I love you, too," echoed from my lips.

What was wrong with me? We renewed our relationship. Again. I believe I felt a lot of guilt from the rape – continuing to see myself as responsible. I looked at myself as damaged goods. Was that the way Christopher viewed me, too? He never wanted to hear me out when I feebly attempted to tell him about Chicago. Now, why was he wanting to continue an affair with me? Perhaps he did care. Really?

For the next days and weeks, upon my return to Michigan, our relationship see-sawed. We went through good times and bad times. Studying, dotted with partying and relaxing, filled the spaces in our lives. We did a lot of things together, but we didn't share anymore like we merrily did when we first met. Yes, we had discussions – many of them. Both Christopher and I were quite the conversationalists. And we surrounded ourselves with people and activities. Words filled with laughs and jokes were always present. From the outside, it must have looked like we were "made for each other" in spite of our cultural, racial, and religious differences. I see now that we really didn't connect in a genuine, honest way – at least I didn't. Months earlier, I opened up to Chris about my haunting Chicago ordeal. And look how that went.

I asked myself why I remained in such an unhealthy situation. I questioned often why I could not seem to stop what we had started – or why I didn't seem to WANT to stop it, even though Chris made me feel like no matter what I did, it always seemed to be the wrong thing.

Christopher graduated from Hope College in May of 1970, and his goal was to continue his education. As for me, having spent many months in California "trying to find myself," I had one semester remaining to complete my bachelor of arts degree. But now was not the time to do it. In my mind, Christopher was my priority. I dropped out of school in support of Christopher financially and in every other way I could. I felt I was doing the "right thing." Up to that point, Chris had been the beneficiary of a United Nation's scholarship for undergraduate degree studies. Upon completion of that program, he was required to return to Cameroon – unless he would be able to arrange enrollment in a graduate studies program.

During that summer of 1970, Chris and I had many discussions strategizing different ways Christopher would be able to remain in the United States. His temporary student visa had expired, and he was required to return home to Cameroon. Because of many immigration laws concerning people with student visas, working was not possible; therefore, Christopher had no way to have any financial resources. Without any money, he could not continue his education, and he would have to return to Cameroon. He was distraught and looked for a solution. Well, Joy could really help with his dilemma.

I don't remember whose idea it was to get married, but that's what happened – we got married. The date was set for January, and we were wed in my parent's home in Springfield, near Battle Creek, Michigan.

My memory of my wedding day was that Christopher did not arrive on time. He called an hour after the ceremony was scheduled to begin and rudely did not give a reason for his lateness – even though I asked him for an explanation. Christopher said he was on his way and to not worry. I did not feel well that day and wondered if I could be pregnant – but I said nothing to Chris about my suspicion. When Christopher arrived, the wedding began. Christopher never explained or apologized to me or my family for his tardiness.

The marriage event was a quiet affair in Dad and Mom's living room in Springfield, outside Battle Creek. A two-tiered wedding cake, with white frosting adorned with tiny pink flowers, graced the dining room table, and the aroma of roasted turkey filled the kitchen. The celebration was quite modest, with only my family and Christopher's best man attending. It was not the glorious wedding I had dreamed of.

From an upstairs room in the manse, I descended the stairway wearing a light blue wedding dress; Mary Ann told me the color blue represented "fidelity and love's purity." I definitely felt it was not the right choice for me, but *big sis* picked it out, and I accommodated her wishes. As I stepped down off the last step and into the living room, I saw Christopher standing at attention in front of our family's beige sectional davenport. He looked a little stiff and slightly uncomfortable in his navy-blue suit. I joined him, and we held hands while my father officiated. My Matron of Honor, Mary Ann, stood beside me. Christopher's Best Man, Harry Moniba, stood beside Chris. Christopher and I exchanged wedding vows – recited one line at a time by each of us – as prompted by the preacher, my dad. In addition to our Honor Attendants, the wedding guests who witnessed the event were my brother Eugene and his wife Mary, my brother Keith, Mary Ann's husband Ken, my nephew Jonathan and niece Kristen. Racing around through the living room and kitchen, adding lots of noise and merriment, were my young nephews, Erik and Joshua, both toddlers. They were having more fun than anyone else. The rings, purchased the week before at the local Thrifty Acres, were presented, and then I fainted.

The nuptials complete, Christopher could legally remain in this country. I wondered if, all along, this had been Christopher's plot for him to stay in the U.S. We moved to East Lansing quite rapidly after our wedding. Christopher was enrolled in a Ph.D. program in anthropology at Michigan State University. Our move was to an apartment in Spartan Village, a MSU married housing complex. I was fortunate, quickly finding a job at the MSU library. And I was correct about my suspicions; we were both thrilled about the coming of our first child.

The first month of married life was a little rocky, for we had Christopher's former roommate, Harry, living with us temporarily.

Having a guest is not an easy thing, especially when you're a new couple adjusting to each other. But it was the African way. I was happy with it, for people around made me happy. It turned out that Harry was a big help to both of us, and he really pulled his weight with living expenses and household chores. Harry, also a graduate student, was hoping to move on to his own place as quickly as possible. But first, he wanted to arrange for his family to join him. Chris and I assisted Harry with the U.S. Immigration negotiations to help make Harry's plans materialize. Weeks after Harry's family arrived from Liberia, they all relocated to Cherry Lane apartments. I enjoyed socializing and getting to know Harry and his family -- his wife Minita and sons Harry, Jr. and Paul. Minita taught me how to make *jollof rice* and other west African dishes. I dreaded seeing them leave our place, for I was aware that when they moved, Christopher would become more difficult to live with. I was happy the Moniba family lived close by.

Our first child, Fitemi, was born in early September in 1971 after more than thirty hours of labor. I beamed with happiness! Christopher had prayed for a son, so he was initially disappointed. Our daughter was so stunning, however, that Christopher's disappointment was short-lived. We christened her with a Cameroonian name: "Fitemi" for star and "Firrida" for beauty – in the oral language of Meta, spoken in Christopher's home village of Njindom. Fitemi Firrida Forgwe was our beautiful, bright little star.

My Ingham Hospital experience with my tiny daughter was a sign of things to come. Why? Fitemi and I were in that hospital room the entire time by ourselves, without my husband, my child's father. Christopher was nowhere around. I had no idea where he was. That behavior had become a pattern.

The evening after a newborn's birth, as a courtesy to the new parents, the hospital would always arrange a special dinner for them. Chris was aware of that dinner, but he did not attend. My physician, Dr. Carol Varner, "stood in" for my husband. She and I shared a delicious lobster feast the day of Fitemi's birth.

The day I was discharged from Ingham General and returned home to Spartan Village, Chris informed me that we had been granted approval to relocate to a larger two-bedroom unit – since our family size increased to three. That was welcomed good news. Since Christopher was absent most days, the responsibility of moving landed on me – a new mom. I took on the job of packing up and moving our things. With the help of the Moniba's, other friends, and my parents, I managed to move our family to a larger flat! I was so thrilled to be a mother. Fitemi added a breath of fresh air to my otherwise stale, troubled life.

Chris and I just existed under the same roof. At least some of the time – for he was absent more than he was present. But at least he developed a loving relationship with Fitemi; he relished playing with her when he was home, tossing her up high and carrying her to and fro on his broad shoulders -- and she loved being around him. He never wanted to talk or help or support me, however. It was my character to make things cheerful and bright, so I constantly continued to be as happy and joyful as I could manage, but it was difficult -- for he took on the role of a potentate. King Christopher ran the household. He took complete control, from the household furnishings to the functions we attended.

The following January, Chris agreed, reluctantly, to move back to Holland so I could finish my last semester at Hope College; we rented an upstairs apartment on the corner of 23rd and College. Chris drove the two-hour trip to East Lansing three times per week to teach an African Art course. I was working, attending my Hope College classes, and caring for Fitemi – four months old at the time. Oftentimes, I carried her to class with me. In one of my biology labs, I brought along an infant seat for her to rest in. A sweet young girl across from our apartment on 23rd Street helped me with child care some of the time; I was also able to occasionally leave little Fitemi with her Great Aunt and Great Uncle Klaaren on 14th Street. Money was tight, but I used my new blender from Mom to make lots of good nutritious meals for my new baby girl. I had a lot on my plate, but I handled the pressure as best I could.

Dealing with Christopher's moods was the greatest stress of all. I recall the day during a college break when I wanted to ride along to class with Christopher. I missed Minita and my other East Lansing friends. I was hoping to see them for just a little while.

When I asked if I could ride along, Christopher yelled: "No. Why would I take you with me when you look like a fucking elephant?"

He struck my back and forced me into the small alcove outside Fitemi's bedroom. He kept pounding me against those stairs in that little dark alcove. He left me there, crying. I soaked my dress all night to get the blood out. I didn't go to my classes for three days – until the bruises faded. Thank God Fitemi was too young to notice.

Chris re-kindled his relationship with Jodi, the daughter of Fitemi's godmother. Jodi, Chris, and I had spent many happy times together two years earlier. But now, half of Christopher's time was spent in East Lansing and the other half in Holland – oftentimes with Jodi. I was no longer included. Chris and I stopped hosting friends at our place. He rarely spent time at home. Fitemi and I were usually by ourselves.

For the first time in my life, I did poorly academically. I couldn't study. I couldn't concentrate. I wanted to have a healthy relationship – one with a mom, a dad, and a child living harmoniously – but my husband was never present to develop any kind of connection. One night, when I was fed up with Christopher's absenteeism, I took Fitemi to my uncle and aunt's house on 14th Street. When Chris got ready to go out, I cheerfully walked out to the car and said I was going to accompany him. I must have been suffering from a very short memory.

Christopher became angry and started insulting me. He got in his big blue Plymouth Fury. Then I got in the Fury. He shrieked at me, pushing me against the passenger door. When I opened my door, he shoved me out. I stood up and defiantly sat on the hood of the car, daring him to leave without me. Chris sped out of the driveway abruptly, and I fell hard onto the driveway, permanently damaging four of my front teeth.

After I graduated from Hope College, we moved back to East Lansing, and Christopher found a job with the Michigan Department of Corrections. Being married to an American citizen, he was now a permanent resident and able to be employed. His position was a unit manager at the Michigan Training Unit, a medium-security prison located in Ionia, Michigan. Ionia was a small town situated between East Lansing and Grand Rapids. Reflecting back, how ironic the situation was that my abusive husband was employed at a prison – and at our home, my husband acted out prison discipline on me.

For the next couple years, we lived in East Lansing at University Village, a married housing complex similar to Spartan Village, where we lived before I finished at Hope College. Chris commuted back and forth from East Lansing to Ionia, and I worked on MSU's campus in the Sociology Department. Chris continued to socialize on his own; I was never included. Then, some new friends entered our lives. One of Christopher's anthropology department classmates, Gerry, had just returned from Cameroon, where he had been conducting anthropological research towards his doctorate. While living in Cameroon, Gerry met and married a Cameroonian woman from Mamfe. He and his wife, Suzanne, moved in across the street from us on campus. Since Chris and I had long stopped going anywhere together, I had forgotten how Christopher treated me in social situations. Gerry and Suzanne regularly invited us to their apartment. One would think that being a guest in a friend's house would bring out good behavior, but no, Chris ordered me around in front of our friends, constantly criticizing me. I remember many occasions when Chris commanded me to take Fitemi home; or to go buy more snacks and drinks. Being ordered around was embarrassing – but I learned that if I didn't follow his instructions, I would have to endure the consequences.

On occasion I drove my trusty old Dodge the two-hour trek to Holland to visit Mom and Dad. Those trips were my way of staying away from Christopher, but I never revealed that to my parents. I could not be honest about my situation. My motive for those visits was more to gain relief than anything else. I also often visited another family on my Holland trips – a family introduced to me by my husband, who met them through a relative working at Hope College. Chris knew the Simpson family, Mattie and Carl, and their nine children, before I did. It seemed ironic that my husband had introduced us and did not continue his amity with them; and now they shared with me a great friendship. The entire family always welcomed me. Carl, in search of more opportunity and a better job, moved his entire family northward from the Kentucky coal mines twenty-plus years earlier. Bobbie, the eldest and probably fifteen years older than me, became like my big sister; she was always kind and helpful to me. Later, I met Pat, another daughter of Carl and Mattie. Pat and I met in 1971 in the Simpson family home on Maple Street in Zeeland; Bobbie introduced us when I was expecting Fitemi. Patricia gave me the first clothing I put on my first child. It was the beginning of a lifelong friendship. We were young moms in our mid-twenties. We spent many hours discussing family issues, politics and civil rights. Pat and I often burned the midnight oil. We were around the same age, and we became friends quickly. We shared a lot of our secrets, and Pat didn't hold back her dislike for my husband.

My friendship with the Simpson family showed me a characteristic of Christopher that I found difficult to believe – his intolerance of African-Americans. Christopher commented to me on more than one occasion that he didn't want me getting too close to the Simpson family – because they were a part of the American Black culture! He reminded me that he was a Cameroonian, a "true African." What an arrogant attitude. I was confused and bewildered. Listening more carefully to the words Chris used, I saw a bigoted and biased side of my husband.

My father taught me at a very early age that all persons have the same rights – no one is better than anyone else, and everyone should be treated fairly and equally. Dad instructed us – me and my siblings – that racist words, attitudes and actions, which exist in ALL people, must be addressed, dealt with honestly, and discarded rapidly. But Christopher thought he was superior in many ways. I questioned what on earth attracted me to him.

Since the forty-five-minute commute from East Lansing to Ionia was inconvenient for Christopher, he decided we should uproot ourselves, leave MSU's campus, and move to Ionia, where Christopher's employment was located. What he said was law. We moved into a large and quite dated apartment on the north side of Ionia; it was on the second floor of a plumbing business. The only access was a rickety outside stairway, badly in need of paint. The yard was full of plumbing supplies. We were a few miles out in the country, north of the town off M-66, with no neighbors except the landlord and his family. Ionia, a small working-class community, was far less accepting of an interracial couple than East Lansing, a more cosmopolitan university town. And guess who was driving forty-plus miles to medical appointments, not to mention the distance to deliver my second child?

Close to the middle of May, I knew it was time. My due date had arrived. Luckily Chris was at work, and could be easily located and summoned. He drove us to East Lansing to drop off Fitemi at Harry and Minita's apartment. We drove to Lansing, and I checked in at St. Lawrence Hospital. Dr. Varner had me whisked down to the X-ray lab because she thought my baby was turned around in the womb. Fortunately, it was a false alarm. My labor was not as long and hard as when Fitemi was delivered. My beautiful son was born naturally, with no medication, and in record time. He was a fine, robust, handsome baby boy. Chris, in an extremely happy frame of mind, named him Bentasi Zikoma – after the oldest, wisest man in the village of Njindom. A male child was exactly what my patrilineal husband had ordered; Christopher was so ecstatic, not to mention overwhelmed and overtaken with pride and joy, that he left me and Bentasi alone in the hospital -- and Chris went out somewhere to celebrate on his own.

Bentasi was only a few months old and Fitemi was almost three. I no longer remember the occasion, but we drove to Detroit to visit our friends, Dembe and Yolanda, whom we met through Harry's family. Dembe, who was from Kenya, had been studying in the States for many more years than Chris. Dembe stood over 6 feet, radiating a fun-loving and accepting disposition. Chris and Dembe became good friends. Yolanda was from Zeeland, a conservative Dutch community about five miles from Holland. She and her five siblings were raised on a large Zeeland farm. Her upbringing, in some ways, was similar to mine. Yolanda was bold and confident. In spite of Yolanda's controlling personality, I rapidly grew to enjoy her company. The four of us became close and trusting. That Detroit visit with our friends broke my trust.

Bentasi woke me up in the middle of the night with diarrhea. He had a stomach ache and soiled the sheets. When I got up to get a wet cloth in the bathroom, I saw Chris talking with Yolanda on the front porch. Dembe was in bed. I changed Bentasi's diaper and rocked him back to sleep. Christopher volunteered to wash out the sheets and diaper. Wow! Could this be true? Chris was helping with the laundry? I lay back down with Bentasi cuddled beside me. I don't know what startled me, but I sat up in bed – and Chris was still not there. Wondering about the front porch scenario I witnessed earlier, I got out of bed to look for my husband. I noticed the basement door ajar, so I began walking down the stairs to check if Chris had finished the laundry. Hearing giggling, Christopher bumped into me as he ran up the stairs – pulling up his pants! Yolanda strolled along behind him.

Startled to see me, Christopher commanded, "Go back to bed – now!!!"

I ran up the stairway, debating whether to wake up Dembe, but I feared a fight between Dembe and Christopher – so I obediently climbed back in bed and cried myself to sleep. The next morning, Yolanda ignored me, and Christopher and I drove home to Ionia in silence. No more was said.

Christopher was rarely home. He routinely left after work, toting his camera gear with him. When he would return, he often spent time with Fitemi and Bentasi. He was gentle and caring with them. Later, when the kids went to bed, Chris frequently worked for hours in his photo darkroom before leaving us and going out who knows where. Becoming more and more skeptical about Christopher's extracurricular activities, one day, I checked out his darkroom when he uncharacteristically forgot to bolt the door. My eyes were drawn to a folder containing photographs of naked women. And Yolanda was one of them! I started to become more aware of his routines.

Garnering up my nerve a bit, one night, I got in my car and followed Christopher. He exited the highway about twenty miles west of Ionia and pulled into a parking lot on the west side of Lowell, near a grocery store. I parked in the lot, quite a distance from his light blue Plymouth sedan. It was dark, so I could not make out the identity of the woman in Christopher's car. As I drove closer, I got a clear view of my friend, Yolanda, wrapped in my husband's arms! Surprising myself, I jumped out of my car, yanked open Christopher's car door, and confronted both of them.

"Oh my God!" I yelled. "What is going on?"

Christopher was hollering, and Yolanda was whimpering. I don't know what they said, as I was not listening to any of it. I stormed away and drove back to Ionia, with Yolanda's car following me closely. She continued following me up my apartment's steps. I don't know why I allowed her in. I was hurt and confused. Yolanda and I were friends. I didn't want to believe she could use my friendship to get involved with my husband. And why would she want to? I felt disillusioned. Yolanda tried to justify her actions. I didn't know where Christopher went. When Yolanda left and walked out of my apartment, I felt kind of empty. I was angry and hurt, but I still wondered what I was doing wrong.

I tried to lose weight and joined a health club in Grand Rapids. Early in October, as I was driving back to Ionia from the gym, a deer crossed the highway in front of me; I tried to swerve, but I hit the deer, forcing the hood of my car to fly up, obscuring my vision. Luckily, I wasn't hurt. The car was inoperable. I had Christopher contacted, and he eventually appeared. It took him hours. My husband was annoyed about the damage I cause to his car.

When Yolanda delivered her second child – a baby boy – Christopher and I drove to Detroit to visit her in the maternity ward. I didn't want to go, and I couldn't understand why Chris wanted me with him. Perhaps he didn't want Dembe to know. Since only immediate relatives were allowed in the ward, Chris and I were denied entry. I thought we would turn around and go back home. But Christopher deceptively passed himself off as Yolanda's pastor – and he visited her while I waited in the parking lot. When Chris returned to the car, he gleefully informed me that Yolanda chose to name her baby boy Danjuma Dembe – "Dembe" named for his father, and "Danjuma," as suggested by Christopher. It made me wonder about little Danjuma's paternity. The true father was never revealed, but I had my suspicions.

It was a stormy evening, and I had just put Fitemi and Bentasi to bed. I cleaned up the dinner dishes, vacuumed the floors, and turned on the stereo. I read late into the evening, finally retiring around midnight. It must have been 3:00 a.m. when I heard Chris come in. I got out of bed and walked into the kitchen. I asked Chris where he had been. No answer. Then I told him that Gerry had called him earlier in the evening. Silence. When I commented that he seemed to be avoiding his long-time buddies – Gerry and Harry, for example – he angrily raised his arm and viciously backhanded me across the face! His ring cut me sharply above my right eye. With blood running down my face, Chris yelled out something about minding my own business. When I reached for the wall phone, Chris grabbed it, fiercely ripping it out of the kitchen wall, with plaster flying everywhere! He stormed out.

The following morning, I packed my things. I gathered the kids and drove to East Lansing to seek help – hoping to locate some of my friends. From Suzanne and Gerry's place, I called a lawyer to ask about my rights; then, I legally separated and moved into Kings Pointe East Apartments in East Lansing. Bentasi was nine months old now, and Fitemi was three.

After a few weeks, Christopher located me. He walked into my apartment, gently picked up Bentasi, and Chris broke into tears. He couldn't handle being separated from his son. I was scared, but at the same time, I felt torn. I feared Chris would hit me for leaving him, but at the same time, I felt badly about separating him from our children.

We continued to live at separate addresses – I lived in East Lansing, and Christopher lived in Ionia. Life was arduous during that period. I was working in the Administration Building at Michigan State, as a statistical typist. The children were cared for at a local daycare center. I couldn't make ends meet, so I applied for public assistance. ADC was granted, and I managed. As time passed, I grew to enjoy my independence. Out from under Christopher's control, I began to resume my old self – pre-Chris. I made friends. I socialized regularly with Suzanne and Gerry in University Village. Suzanne loved to tell Cameroonian folktales to Fitemi and Bentasi. Suzanne and I became very close. She confided in me, relaying how sad she was that Gerry's parents would not accept her – a Cameroonian woman. She was well aware of my situation. She advised me to leave Chris permanently. Suzanne was ashamed to be from the same country as Christopher. Harry and Minita often invited me over for dinner and socializing. They helped me a lot with Fitemi and Bentasi. Harry and Minita, too, advised me to divorce Christopher. Harry knew how unfaithful, abusive, and irresponsible Chris was. I often drove to Holland to visit my parents – and I would always spend time with my friend, Patricia. She, too, told me what I didn't want to hear.

Spring came, and I visited my friend, Jil, in Marne. Jil was married to Adam, Yolanda's brother. It was stormy that night, with lots of thunder and lightning. While I was at Jil's house, I noticed one of Christopher's denim button-down shirts hanging in Jil's kitchen. Puzzled, I asked her how it got there. Jil thought the shirt was Yolanda's shirt – since Yolanda had it on the day she last visited Marne. Suspicions mounted, but the storm hastened me home. The kids and I were soaked from the rainfall as we ran to the car. The ride home seemed endless. Approaching my apartment building, I saw my neighbors sitting out in the stairwell. My apartment windows were all steamed up. The rainstorm had caused sporadic flooding in my area near the Grand River. I soon discovered my basement apartment had flooded. I cleaned up as best I could, but many of my things were damaged and not salvageable. My parents and my friends Harry and Gerry helped me relocate into another apartment in the same complex. I settled in but was afflicted with extreme fatigue. I kept working, but my energy level was steadily dwindling.

It was six weeks later, around Bentasi's first birthday, that I became very ill. I was diagnosed with hepatitis. Dr. Varner believed I contracted the disease cleaning up my apartment, which had been flooded with contaminated water from the Grand River. My doctor advised me to stop breast feeding Bentasi immediately. I was admitted to St. Lawrence Hospital, and the kids went to Holland to stay with their grandparents. Christopher didn't visit me very often. I wondered how he was spending his time. Why wouldn't he take care of Fitemi and Bentasi? I was in the hospital for one month.

When I was discharged from St. Lawrence Hospital, Chris and I reunited. I don't remember why I agreed to try again. I was still quite sick, so perhaps I was vulnerable. We rented a small house on Collingwood, in East Lansing – near the Collingwood entrance to campus. Things were calm and quiet for a short time, for we were very busy with two lively youngsters -- but before long, the unwanted old patterns returned.

But things were looking up. I applied and obtained a great position as the Office Manager for Michigan State's Department of Physics and Astronomy. It was a great job. I loved it. At least I didn't have to commute from Ionia. That position provided me with the will to function again. Without any emotional support from my husband, at least I was receiving some kudos from work. My position provided me with the strokes I was lacking at home. At my new job, I was respected and commended. I performed my duties well. But home life did not change.

One morning, I got up early to do our accumulated laundry. While I sorted through the mountains of clothes, I discovered a photograph in the pocket of one of Christopher's trousers. It stunned me. It was a photo of Yolanda wearing a Cameroonian yellow and blue beaded necklace – the one given to me by Chris. I delayed the laundering and drove to work in a cloud of anger mixed with hurtfulness. I had trouble concentrating on work tasks throughout the entire morning. In the middle of the day, I told my supervisor that I felt ill, and I left before the workday was over. As I drove into our driveway, I saw Christopher's red Karmann Chia parked out front in the street. I questioned why he would be home in the middle of the day. As I walked through the front door, I saw Christopher standing there in front of me, naked and holding a wine glass in each hand. He quickly dropped the goblets and stepped toward me, grabbing my arms and shoving me up the stairs. Chris held me securely at the top of the stairway, enabling whomever was in the family room downstairs to exit unseen. Minutes later, he released me from his grip and hurried to his car in the street. I ran downstairs to take a look, but they had already left. I cleaned up the broken glass and changed the locks. It didn't keep him out. He broke in through the dining room window.

Over the next year, Christopher and I continued to grow farther apart. I was working and basically supporting us, for Chris did his own thing and used his resources to support his toys – his sporty car, cameras, and photography equipment, a motorcycle, and varied art supplies.

I continued to question why I could not bring myself to leave Christopher. I knew I would be able to support myself. But I was brought up to believe marriage was a lifelong commitment -- and that if I was patient, things would get better. In addition, haunting my mind was a lot of guilt and shame stemming from my Chicago ordeal years earlier. How could I be so stupid, I thought.

I could have handled Christopher's embellishment of his childish toys, but his aggression, violence, and betrayal were too much. Added to all of that, it became apparent that he was involved with yet another woman, in addition to Yolanda. One of Christopher's colleagues at work, Liam, and his wife, Elaine, were a couple we met and went to dinner with a month earlier. I was unaware of the relationship between Elaine and Chris. She and her husband, along with Chris and me, occasionally socialized. Elaine sometimes played her guitar at a small bar in Fowler, a little village near Ionia. On a few occasions, we listened and enjoyed her music. One spring day in May, we invited Liam and Elaine to accompany us to my parent's home in Holland to visit the annual Tulip Festival. I remember ignoring signs of affection between Chris and Elaine. Elaine was newly pregnant, and I recall her suffering from some minor nausea at the Saturday parade. Shortly after our Holland trip, I lost contact with Elaine and Liam. I tried to telephone Elaine, but she ignored my calls. Months later, some friends who knew Elaine and Liam visited me. I asked them how Elaine's pregnancy was progressing.

Immediately, I sensed an aura of awkwardness and discomfort. They said Elaine had recently given birth to a baby girl, but they didn't know any more about it.

I tried to guess what they meant. Their words rolled around in my mind, and I wondered why Elaine had not informed me of her child's birth. What was she hiding? I decided to seek out some information. I left work early and drove to Elaine and Liam's house in Fowler. No one was home. Occasionally, I had visited with Elaine's mother, Joan, so I went to Joan's place hoping to find some answers. When Joan opened the door, I wasn't sure how I would come up with the words to ask her all the questions floating around in my head – but it didn't matter. Joan started talking. She hugged me and began crying. Joan offered me a cup of coffee, and we sat down at her little kitchen table. She said that Elaine was in the house but that she was too sick with depression to get out of bed. Joan wept as she divulged her daughter's ordeal. Joan's words were filled with raging anger at Christopher's and Elaine's deceitful behavior. I was wrapped in a cloud of shock as Joan told me that her new granddaughter could not be Elaine and Liam's child – for the sweet little girl's olive skin tone and curly hair revealed a father other than Liam. Joan felt that Elaine, afflicted with depression and epilepsy, was not well enough to care for her child, and Joan conveyed that she and her husband were not equipped to raise their granddaughter. They didn't think they could handle raising a bi-racial child in their conservative little town.

Elaine and Christopher's newborn baby girl was made available for adoption, and Liam proceeded to divorce Elaine. Liam was granted full custody of Liam and Elaine's five-year-old daughter.

Concurrently with Christopher's involvement with Elaine, Chris and Yolanda met secretly at various hotels and out-of-the-way places – from Zeeland to Grandville to Borculo. Yolanda eventually became pregnant; but she honestly did not know if the father of her child was Christopher or Dembe. My friend Pat helped open my eyes to the existence of that uncertainty. I didn't want to believe it. When the relationship between Yolanda and Christopher became known to all involved parties, Dembe went berserk – and he threatened to kill Chris. After all, Christopher and Dembe had been "best buddies."

Dembe confronted the situation head-on. He called me and asked if I would be so kind as to be at my parent's place that evening for an important meeting. I was very fearful of what would happen. He explained himself and said he was going to call my husband, too. Dembe then phoned Chris at work and told him that he wished to discuss "what the hell" was going on – he wanted to know the nature of the relationship between Yolanda and Christopher. Dembe proceeded to instruct Christopher to be at MY parent's house at 7:00 p.m. sharp. Dembe knew my dad, and liked him; a referee was what I think Dembe desired. What an ordeal! It was Christmas vacation. My sister and her husband were visiting with their son, Erik. My brother-in-law, Ken, was lying flat on his back on the living room floor of Mom and Dad's place. Ken was unable to move around because of a painful slipped disk in his back.

I will never forget that Christmas-time evening. Mom, Dad, Chris, Dembe, Yolanda, and I all went out and sat on the front porch. The tension on that porch was at the breaking point. Christopher senselessly tried to make some amusing jokes. Then Dembe asked Yolanda to speak. Yolanda poured her heart out, revealing that she and Chris had been secretly meeting for two years. She told about places they had arranged private meetings, including her parent's barn on their Zeeland farm. Dembe tried to attack Chris, but Dad held him back. I was in shock.

Then Chris spoke: "I have **never** had any involvement with Yolanda. She is lying about everything!"

I was jolted by Christopher's lies. I didn't think it could get any worse, but it did. Yolanda threatened to find a gun and shoot Christopher right before he jumped up and stormed out. Dembe stared at Yolanda, not knowing what to say. Then Yolanda left, and Dad followed her – perhaps for her protection and safety. I sat there in Mom's antique oak rocker, trembling, not knowing what to do next. My world had been shaken to its core.

The following week, I moved, with my children, to Edgewood Village in East Lansing. My parents, Harry and Minita, and Gerry and Suzanne, helped me with the relocation. Dembe insisted that Christopher's blood be tested for the paternity misgivings of Yolanda's unborn child. I was told the tests revealed Chris was not the father, but I'm not sure about that. I didn't want Christopher anywhere around me. I had tolerated enough. I was scared of him – he was so unpredictable.

But I still wondered if there was something I was doing wrong. And then, after settling into my Edgewood Village apartment, I discovered I was pregnant – for the third time! Even though Chris had damaged many people's lives, I wondered how I would manage with three children by myself.

We had separated and re-united three times over the last seven years. Christopher was becoming more unsettled and restless, smoking more and more weed. In the summer of 1977, he announced to me that it was time for him to go home to Cameroon, along with his family, of course. Even though Chris had damaged many people's lives, I still allowed him back into mine. Why didn't I have any respect for myself?

I think I fantasized that Christopher would miraculously transform when he returned to Cameroon, his beloved homeland. He would be oceans away from Yolanda and Elaine and Jodi and whomever else had come between us. I felt he needed to touch base with his family in Cameroon. I agreed to accompany him. What was I thinking?

Winter ended, and spring and summer came and went with all kinds of tasks related to the big relocation to Cameroon. My pregnancy was progressing normally, and Fitemi and Bentasi were exhibiting excitement about having a new little sister or brother. I was a bit worried about traveling in my advanced pregnant state, but my doctor assured me there was nothing to be concerned about.

The planning and preparation continued. The next few months involved tickets, passports, vaccinations, selling our cars, and many more details for a trip across continents. When monies from the Cameroonian government arrived for our travels, it really hit me that I would be leaving everything familiar to me. And because of my husband's behaviors and actions, I knew that my family had doubts, my friends had doubts, and many others had doubts about the wisdom of me and the kids accompanying Christopher to Cameroon. I had doubts, too, but I was silent – for I was excited. Wow – the trip of a lifetime. Fitemi and Bentasi, anticipating an adventure, could not stop talking about airplanes and flying.

Autumn leaves were falling, and Dad was vigorously raking when we arrived. I grabbed a rake to assist Dad, and then he strolled over to give Fitemi and Bentasi a big bear hug. Their grandpa laughed and giggled with them, raking a huge pile of leaves into a mountain for jumping in and out of. What fun! Temi and Tasi sure adored Grandpa.

Mom had started supper. She prepared a chuck roast in her trusty wrought iron Dutch oven. I smelled it from out in their yard. We were anticipating quite a treat. When the kids ran in after playing in the leaves, they went right to Grandma's cookie jar – the one with the tiny red cherries – to grab some goodies. Grandma stopped them, exclaiming, "wait 'til after supper, sweeties." We ate and stayed overnight at Mom and Dad's place, preparing to leave for Cameroon the following morning.

Shortly after supper, Christopher went out. He left early in the evening. I didn't know why or where for he said nothing as he walked out the door. I wasn't going to let anything spoil my adventuresome trip. In the morning, while enjoying Dad's blueberry pancakes, I heard my mother whispering to Dad that Chris didn't return until dawn. I ignored Mom.

We rode in silence – except for Fitemi and Bentasi's giggling and laughing -- from Holland to the municipal airport in Lansing. We unloaded the car and sauntered inside to check-in. After we were all set, Christopher walked away to somewhere in the terminal. What!?! The departure of the plane was delayed, waiting for the one remaining passenger – my husband! I was embarrassed and boarded alone with the kids. Christopher made it to the plane just before takeoff – barely.

Arriving at the Detroit Metropolitan airport, the attendant at the check-in counter informed us that our luggage exceeded the weight limit. Now what? We opened our suitcases and discarded many of our belongings – to bring down the poundage under the baggage weight limit. We kept the photos and tossed the album covers, kept the nicest clothing, and tossed my faded dresses and worn-out shoes; we basically kept what Chris wanted and threw out what Chris didn't want. Since many of my things were pitched, I felt brushed aside. That was not the way I had planned to begin our trans-Atlantic journey.

CHAPTER 4

Charming 1970's Cameroon

Humid, hot air squeezed me like a wet glove as I stepped off the plane and onto the tarmac in Douala, Cameroon's largest city. Fortunately, the long international flight failed to coax my body into premature labor contractions, but the heat glued my wet brown hair to my neck and back. In spite of Mother Nature's discomforts, I was overflowing with cheerfulness and anticipation. Fitemi and Bentasi pulsated with twelve hours of stored-up energy, ready to run and play. Their young eyes opened wide as they gazed out over the brightly dressed folks bustling about the seaport. Another plane had to be boarded *super vite* – so my glimpse of the bustling port city was over in an instant. We made our way to Yaoundé, Cameroon's capital city, located in the equatorial zone of the African continent.

I was shocked no one met us. How could someone be gone for more than ten years and not be met by his family? I think I had expected some sort of reception or welcome-back festivity; after all, it had been more than a decade since Christopher walked on Cameroonian soil. Back in 1967, 24-year-old Christopher won a United Nations "African

Studies Programs through American Universities" (ASPAU) scholarship, which landed him at Hope College in Holland, Michigan. After four years of college and six years of graduate studies, he was returning home with an American wife, a five-year-old daughter, a three-year-old son, and another child on the way. Was there no one who wanted to welcome him home?

I began to realize that Christopher had notified no one of our arrival. I never understood why Chris insisted on leaving Michigan in such a hurry. Was there a reason he didn't inform any of his friends or family? Why did we leave Michigan before he researched and wrote his dissertation – with all the coursework done except for the closure needed for a Ph.D. to be granted? What could the reason be?

Christopher was back home, but he looked lost. Convincing the airport officials that he was a Cameroonian proved difficult. We were in East Cameroon, in the city of Yaoundé, a place Christopher was not acquainted with. The language spoken was French and Chris was not fluent.

Christopher grew up in West Cameroon when East Cameroon and West Cameroon had separate governments – and different official languages. The English-speaking West, approximately one-fifth of the country, had its own prime minister until 1970. Yaoundé, in French-speaking East Cameroon, was almost as new for Chris as for me. We sat for hours in Yaoundé's airport, going through the many dreaded customs requirements and rituals. Chris was annoyed with all the red tape, and his elementary French language skills made things worse.

As we left the airport, the warm breeze outside felt soothing – a pleasant relief from Douala' closeness. The four of us piled into a yellow taxicab. The taxi driver, refusing to acknowledge that Chris was from Cameroon, tried to charge us a "foreign" rate, which was a higher price for ignorant tourists. Following a fervent discussion, the driver conceded to accept the normal fare, but he delayed again when Chris paid him in dollars. After lots of name-calling and four-letter expletives, we were on our way. Peering through the taxi window, I wondered when we would arrive in Yaoundé proper.

Motoring the roads was like an obstacle course – winding in and out around potholes strategically scattered across the roadways – at a speed I don't care to remember. Bentasi and Fitemi thought it was great fun – much like a joy-ride at Cedar Point. I was still wondering when we would arrive in Yaoundé. Chris told me we were already in Yaoundé, and I felt the onset of culture shock!

I assumed we were in the open countryside – not a city. Enormous gullies lined most of the roads. Rows of rudimentary flat-roofed buildings alongside the streets were surrounded by children playing, adults working and conversing, and some women cooking. Many rooftops were covered with clothes spread out haphazardly to dry. Scrawny goats and pigs wandered around freely – and mangy wild dogs scrounged through the piles of roadside rubbish.

Yet the sun was shining brightly, and colorful flowers bloomed everywhere. Having grown up in Iowa, I never realized what palm trees looked like, and now I was seeing hundreds of them in a variety of shapes and sizes -- they graced the countryside all over the place. Some of the larger palms doubled as urinals. As we approached the heart of Yaoundé, activities spiraled dramatically. Hand-painted, carved signs were flaunted across the faces of most storefronts -- in a variety of languages. Open-air markets enticed swarms of people and undertakings. Vibrantly painted vans and trucks whizzed in and out and across the intersections as if all the vehicles were involved in a race – competing with the fast-moving, wildly driven yellow taxicabs.

On both sides of the roadways, there were throngs of people walking and biking and laughing. On the side streets, young boys playfully pursued the slower-moving vehicles, springing on and off their bumpers. Women and children were brilliantly draped in beautiful fabrics – many wore stunning batiks that flowed from head to toe. Blended throughout the crowds were a few folks wearing typical western clothing. A full-color portrait of Cameroon's long-reigning president, Ahidjo, was brightly printed on the fabric of some young men's dashikis. Many women, and a few brave men, balanced baskets or pots on their heads. Children's crowns were piled high with schoolbooks.

As young women in spiked heels gingerly strolled by, I wondered how they managed to traverse those muddy, rutted walkways. Street vendors displayed their wares alongside the crumbling streets – yummy-looking treats unfamiliar to me but bursting with pungent aromas. Some young Cameroonians sported *Levis,* others *Lees.* The variety was incredible – and wonderful.

As we drew near to the center of Yaoundé, fast-beating soulful music from drums, tambourines and maracas radiated from crowded city crooks and corners. Everything, and everyone, was so alive. The city was pulsating with activity. A fresh new world was invading my senses. I wanted to experience it all.

I asked my husband lots of questions, but he was distant, not wanting to converse. His body language showed a concern for where we were going to sleep that night. Well – no one knew we were coming.

Fitemi and Bentasi were tired and hungry. With an abundance of vendors flooding the walkways, we stopped to buy some spicy grilled fish and koki – a sweet pudding made from black-eyed peas or accra beans wrapped and baked in plantain leaves. A few hours later, Christopher located a dingy cheap hotel, and we checked in – exhausted.

The second-floor hotel room was dark and sparsely furnished. There was only one bed, with no sheets or bedding of any kind. The bed was crude – wired springs graced with a lumpy mattress, which sagged when I sat on it. A wobbly open shelf contained sheets and towels, all dingy and tattered. No chairs or places to put anything. Christopher checked out the bathroom, complaining about the stained sink.

Then he raised his voice and gave orders. "Joy, bathe the kids. Unpack the suitcases. Make up the beds."

As I carried out his commands, I wondered why I felt so obliged to obey. Was I terrified of his temper? Was I being a "good wife" based on my Bible-belt culture? As I unpacked our luggage in that sleazy hotel room, I couldn't help remembering another room in Chicago a decade ago. Responding to my husband's commands, I unpacked the children's suitcases and looked for their pajamas. Chris washed in the bathroom. I helped Fitemi and Bentasi clean up and get ready for bed. Bentasi, a very sensitive child, was crying that he wanted to see Grandpa Klaaren. Fitemi, a curious five-year-old, overflowed with excitement about what the next morning would bring. I dozed off between them, falling asleep in my street clothes – too exhausted to undress.

Somewhat refreshed by a full night's sleep, I sat up and noticed the daylight opening its eyelids. Similar to my daughter, I was eager to go outside and view our unique surroundings. I jumped up out of bed and opened the room's only window. Light flowed in and took possession of the entire space. Beaming with excitement, I encouraged my family to hurry so we could continue our exploration of that new land. Almost ready to go, I was frustrated that my left shoe was missing. How could I go out and explore with only one shoe?

During a long search for the missing shoe, my husband's aggression grew and exploded. I was ridiculed and shamed, instructed to take responsibility for "my big mistake" – losing my shoe. And furthermore, I was blamed for forcing us to spend money buying another pair. I wondered what would happen next. I should have packed more shoes, but then I recalled how we threw out many of our possessions, including shoes, in the Detroit airport.

Nothing to be upset about. I had become a master rationalizer for survival. My emotions had been pulled, pushed, squeezed beyond my own recognition. Was I required to remember and take care of all details? The hours spent organizing, shopping, and childcare. Shots, visas, passports, exchange rates, photos, getting addresses, giving addresses, explaining our hurried exit, half-explaining, not explaining. Oh, and by the way, I was expecting my third child. How I completed all the logistics of our journey, I will never know. Was it fear? Was it duty? Was it stupidity?

But there I was in a low-life hotel, wondering where in the hell my shoe had disappeared to. I couldn't go out to explore the city without two shoes. Christopher walked out the door with Fitemi and Bentasi to find me a new pair.

I waited in the hotel, stretched out on the bed, studying the ceiling. Cockroaches were flying about; wall geckos made themselves at home above me; the heat was radiating like mid-August in Hades. First, I melted in Douala. Then, I was put on hold in Yaoundé. No one met us. What was going on? I sat there and sulked in a sagging bed in a filthy hotel room in a city I hadn't seen yet. Nowhere to bathe. My husband seemed restless. He was distant from me. God, what had I gotten myself into?

Hours later, Chris returned with a new pair of shoes. The shoes were not my size, but my "sense of rationalization" made the shoe tightness less uncomfortable.

After searching for living-quarters for days, Chris was contacted by an entourage of young men from Bamenda, Christopher's home in the Northwest Province. That small convoy from West Cameroon brought the great news that we would be lodged with the Muna's – a fellow family from Njindom. The Muna family was part of the former government of West Cameroon. Mr. Muna had been the Prime Minister of West Cameroon before the east and west united in 1970. Then he became head of the General Assembly and re-located to Yaoundé in East Cameroon. Mr. Muna was from Christopher's home village. We now had a place to rest and feel welcomed, if only temporarily. I was ready to vacate that hotel.

When we arrived at the Muna estate, I felt like I was in a storybook movie. The people, the grounds, the dwellings – everything and everyone, exquisite. The front of the hacienda was brimming with burgeoning flowers sporting a rainbow of textures and colors. I enjoyed the red and yellow-lined blooms that looked like a bird's beak; and many large daisy-type flowers in a variety of pink and mauve-like tones. Winding footpaths circled landscaped gardens and fountains. Palms and foliage of many varieties adorned the entire place. Large trees bearing fat, ripe mangoes lined the backside of the acreage. My ambivalent feelings were momentarily soothed. We spent more than a week with Mr. and Mrs. Muna. They were gracious and kind. I can remember Mrs. Muna's scrumptious pound cake melting in my mouth. It was the rest and stability we needed – however short-lived. After our stay at the Muna's ended, it seemed Fitemi and Bentasi had a distorted sense of life in a developing country. For children, it was difficult to understand being deprived when they had just experienced affluence.

Arrangements were made for us to stay in an area called Bastos, in the flat of Humphrey, one of Mr. Muna's sons. Since Humphrey was on business in Switzerland for a month, we were able to temporarily reside there. The main living room space was incredibly modern, with a white low-to-the-floor contemporary couch that had clean lines bordered with light teakwood and stone accents. Two end tables displayed stainless steel and chrome-like accents. Everything was lovely and fashionable. Entering the kitchen, however, was another story; it was quite simple and definitely not functional. On the back porch was a washtub, where laundry had to be hand-scrubbed and hung outside. We enjoyed the surroundings, but our main job was to walk all over Yaoundé, pushing our dossiers in the faces of various government ministries, hoping to find employment. That routine went on for weeks. We eventually ran out of energy and money. And I would soon be due to deliver my third child.

In spite of the uncertainty, those first months in Cameroon were pleasurable for me, exploring and experiencing a new world. I spent many hours experiencing the life and culture there. The lack of skyscrapers was, for me, quite expected. Actually, their absence was a bit refreshing. Yet Yaoundé was speckled with quite a few architectural wonders, but most structures were small one-story buildings often rising out of un-terraced ground, precariously balanced on very hilly terrain, and sometimes surrounded by huge, often impassable, ditches – gullies suggestive of nature taking her course – as if oblivious to the multitudes of people packed into the city. Muddy roads snaked in and out, bearing no discernable pattern – stocked full of water, ruts, and cracks.

Swarms of gleeful children, many pushing their hand-made toy "sticks-and-wheels," played in the market areas. Colors bloomed from the flowing fabrics and the deep green foliage. The sun was sweltering and radiant. Even after the rains, the sunshine would quickly return – in full power.

Cameroonians really enjoyed meeting new friends and sharing meals. When visiting someone's abode, abundant food, drink, and congeniality would flow from everyone's pores. Some specialties were sangha, a mixture of cassava, palm nut juice, and maize; koki, made from black-eyed peas and palm oil; achu, from cocoyams and fufu; and egusi soup, from ground pumpkin seeds and leafy greens or okra. Folks were generous and shared their food and drink and conversation joyfully with all visitors.

Temperature-wise, Yaoundé was marvelously comfortable all year 'round. Although it's a city located in the equatorial zone, Yaoundé sits at a relatively high altitude, enabling the thermometer to span a range from 75 to 85 degrees Fahrenheit.

Cameroon was home to hundreds of languages and many ethnic groups of people – from the Pygmy to the Bantu to the Fulani. Even though both French and English were official languages in Cameroon, many seasoned Cameroonians preferred the languages of their ancestors. I had not yet traveled to Njindom, the village home of Christopher, but I knew the language spoken there was called Meta. Both Fitemi and Bentasi have Meta names. Only a few kilometers away from Njindom, Bafut was spoken. Pidgin English was used extensively – a tool to communicate in spite of the many assorted dialects.

I recall the little shops christened with unique signs – *"Heaven's End"* or *"LA Snow."* Those names seemed illogical, not making a lot of sense; however, they radiated a whimsical and lackadaisical mood. All sorts of wares were spread out in front of the shops, from heavy wrought-iron fences and gates to cooking pots to myriads of baskets in all varieties.

Motoring the bumpy roads took skill – and patience. Lots of ruts and holes. Multitudes of folks walking, biking, traversing into the quartiers, maneuvering around throngs of goats and chickens. The markets – wow – really organic smells. Luckily, I grew up in the Iowa farmland; my background had accustomed me to some of those market odors. Meats hung up for examination and purchase. Chickens still clucking. Rice. Yams. Plantains. Bananas. Mangoes. Papaya. Palm wine. Radiant fabrics. I immersed myself in Cameroonian culture – the dancing, the partying, the celebrating, and the feasting. People knew how to savor life.

My own experience, growing up as a preacher's kid in '50's and '60's small-town America, was far removed from that of the continent I was becoming acquainted with. It was nearing Christmas in Yaoundé, yet the earth was green and the air warm. Fruits and vegetables and other succulent edibles were bountiful, and vibrant foliage graced the countryside.

It didn't take long for me to perceive the overwhelming poverty. What struck me, though, was not the lack of material goods – but the fact that most folks were content living life without the frills of a more resource-rich society; they were living life fully in spite of their relatively meager accommodations. Community and family were paramount. I felt embarrassed, coming from the U.S., where I had so many resources and opportunities at my disposal – and taking them for granted, not fully appreciating them. Life in Cameroon showed me the benefits of living more simply.

My experience was somewhat unique, being married to a Cameroonian. It gave me an advantage over many other foreigners. As part of the Cameroonian family, I was treated respectfully – especially when my children were with me. For example, when taking a taxi alone, the drivers charged me more (American or European prices) until I told them I was married to a Cameroonian from Northwest Province (and had Cameroonian children) – the discount in the taxi fare seemed to be proportional to the number of Cameroonian kids one had!

Whatever path I walked in Yaoundé, people were very courteous. Everyone took time to greet me and talk and laugh. Young women were usually surrounded with small children – and many carried infants on their backs. It was commonplace for mothers to nurse their babies while vending their homemade products or waiting in line in the market. Colorful flowing fabrics – wrapped around as skirts and stacked up as turbines –dazzled in the sun. Hosts of bicycles – many heaped high with colorful cargoes and some transporting fresh loaves of French bread – moved rapidly down the paths and roadways.

Yaoundé city folks asked me endless questions about the United States. Cameroonians were amazed with how informally Americans dressed. In Cameroon people dressed very formally, almost ceremoniously. It seemed rather odd since it was difficult to walk on the rut-ridden streets in fancy clothing and high heels!

There were opportunities to express my own culture, but I tried to minimize them. U.S. Embassy employees spent many hours at the American Club – an affluent "piece of America" where members devoured hamburgers and french fries, played bridge, slurped Manhattans, and swam in the club pool all day and night – with scantily paid young Cameroonian workers serving food and drink and minding the American mothers' children. I found that many Americans working in Cameroon (with the exception of the Peace Corps volunteers) had a tendency to separate themselves from Cameroonian culture. I felt they were selling themselves short, and on a few occasions when my friends and I visited the club, I suggested to a few of the American Embassy personnel that it would be wise and enlightening to immerse themselves and experience the diversity of the culture they were living in.

For me, Cameroon was a fresh new world where people lived modestly and relished life in the present. I wondered why my husband was so different from his countryfolk. How did he develop that way? Cameroonian folks operated cheerfully and calmly – and joyfully lived their lives. They needed few possessions to be content.

Since we were unsuccessful in the job market, we had used all our funds, and I was close to my due date. Chris planned for us to move to Kumba, to Grace and Nick Fominyon's place, Christopher's sister and brother-in-law. Kumba, a four to five-hour drive from Yaoundé and accessible by train, was a small town in West Cameroon. I looked forward to the chance to meet Christopher's siblings.

Grace was tall and dignified. I pictured her as the most stately of the Forgwe women; she was cordial, charming, and attractive. Her voice was well-defined – deep and lovely and strong. Her doting husband, Nick, clearly adored her. Grace and Nick's six spirited, lively children – Evelyn, Alvin, Edwin, Valentine, Henry, and little Irene – ranged from around ten years old down to 8 months. Nick and Grace really had their hands full, but they were overjoyed to accommodate us despite the size of their family. Fitemi and Bentasi spent many hours playing and cavorting with their newly met cousins. It was such a happy time for all of the Forgwe family members.

Nicholas, a teacher at the Government Technical College in Kumba, studied in Pennsylvania a few years before Christopher attended Hope College in Michigan. We all enjoyed getting to know and cherish Nick and Grace and their wonderful family. Both Nick and Grace worked long hours every day – both of them doing so much more than was imaginable by an outsider like me – for shopping had to be done multiple times daily at local markets. Grace worked long hours everyday cooking, laundering, and marketing. The food preparation took hours, since foods were not neatly packaged as in the U.S., And the laundry was done by hand, as I mentioned when we batched at Humphrey's place in Bastos. In most cases, bar soap, cold water, and washboards were utilized. Every piece had to be hung somewhere outdoors. In many cases, roofs would be blanketed with everyone's clothes basking in the sun. And then, after the clothing dried, each item, including and especially underwear, had to be ironed in order to kill certain parasites. Daily life was harsh. Many children performed difficult chores. There was no television, and telephones were available only at certain worksites. It was like going back in time – much farther back than was in my own memory.

Brother Nick went out of his way to ensure everything was comfortable for me during our time in Kumba. Trying to accommodate my very pregnant state, Nick offered to go out and buy a fan so I would be more comfortable. I let him know how much I appreciated his efforts, but I told him I could manage. He took us on some outings – we saw huge African elephants! The kids, of course, were thrilled. Grace prepared countless delicious Cameroonian meals for us -- achu prepared with dried fish using palm oil, corn fufu, fried plantains, and coco-yams, eaten with a tasty stew. Food preparation took a major part of every day. The enjoyment and nourishment were definitely worth waiting for.

Nick arranged for us to travel northward to Buea, which was located at a high altitude – at the foot of Mount Cameroon. We voyaged via auto through the hot and dry Kumba area to the much cooler, highest elevation in West Africa – more than 13,000 feet. Compared to Kumba, it was welcomely comfortable – a little break from the dry heat.

All of us were thrilled to meet Primus, MaryAnn, and Martin, Christopher's younger brothers and sister. Primus worked in the Archives Department in Buea. He had a very gregarious disposition. We liked each other right away; we were about the same age and enjoyed each other's company immediately. He was tall and slender, garnishing a kind and warm personality. Primus was so much fun to be with. Fitemi and Bentasi were drawn to their Uncle Primus instantly.

Then we met MaryAnn, Christopher's youngest sister, who was still a teenager. She and I connected straight away, embracing as if we were long-lost sisters. At the young age of eighteen years, MaryAnn was very cheerful, accommodating, and helpful. Her giggling, happy disposition was contagious. She was staying with her brother Primus while preparing to take two advanced-level exams in January. MaryAnn was a lovely young woman, extremely warm and caring. To celebrate our arrival in Buea, she prepared a delicious breakfast of scrambled eggs and tomatoes, fried plantains, and French bread.

Later in the day, we were delighted to meet Martin, the "baby" of the family. He was mature for his young age and very considerate and gracious. Martin was attending a pre-seminary school outside of Buea; he had already decided that he wanted to become a Roman Catholic priest. He was only sixteen! Martin was cheerful, thoughtful, and serious and seemed willing to take the assignment of arbitrating any Forgwe family disputes or disagreements – in spite of his youthful position in the family. Chris mentioned to me that he was a lot like Martin. However, I saw no traits in Christopher – in behavior or character – that resembled his younger brother.

After our visit in Buea ended, Nicholas returned all of us to Kumba. The climate had remained the same – it was still extremely blisteringly hot. And my advanced pregnant state made me very wearisome. The plan – made and designed by Chris – was for me to deliver my child in Kumba Hospital and have Grace assist me. I was pleased with the proposition, but it was only a projected strategy. I was quite anxious about birthing in Cameroon. I had experienced difficulties delivering my first two children back in Michigan – an extremely long and hard labor with Fitemi and a presumed breach with Bentasi, which turned out to be a false alarm. And now I was in a new place, not known to me, and without a damn doctor! I prayed everything would go smoothly. But the heat was unbearable.

Assuming there was time before I would deliver, we took a short trip to meet Rose Ake, another of Christopher's sisters. Chris described her as the most like Mama Forgwe. A take-charge person, Rose had managed to accumulate opportunities for advanced training and education; at a very young age, Rose traveled to England to study nursing. She was in England when Christopher left for the United States, so they had not connected for more than twelve years. Rose and her husband and children entertained us graciously. One thing I remember was that Rose had a very large ceiling fan in the middle of their living room. I had never seen that in Cameroon! It was so refreshing.

As we returned to Kumba, I again felt the warmth and dryness of that part of Cameroon. I was very much looking forward to seeing more of the Cameroonian countryside, for Christopher told me that the area he was from – the grasslands of Bamenda – was cool and breezy. But I knew that Cameroon also had tropical rainforests and hot, dry deserts. Cameroon's terrain was varied and diverse, almost bewitching.

On New Year's Eve, having resided in Kumba for about a month, I was informed via *Radio Cameroon* that I was offered an employment position with the Government of Cameroon. Holy Cow! Was this really happening?

The procedure in Cameroon was to announce government positions over the radio. Resident addresses did not exist, and television had not as yet come to Cameroon, so radio announcements were the only avenue for dispensing information. It seemed somewhat logical. Anyway, it was announced over the radio that *"Madame Forgwe had been offered a position as a career counselor with the Ministry of Education in Yaoundé – and was to report immediately."*

Labor contractions began on New Year's Day. Grace accompanied me, and I spent three or four hours in the hospital in Kumba, hoping to deliver my baby with Grace as my midwife. However, my child did not cooperate and was not yet ready to enter the world. Dismayed and disgruntled, we all went back to Grace and Nick's place.

Because of my job assignment, we left Kumba that same day. The train ride from Kumba to Douala to Yaoundé was a bit rushed – plus the train de-railed! What!?! We survived that mishap and got on our way about three hours later. Other passengers informed me that derailments there were a common occurrence.

We made it to Yaoundé and found that many documents had to be authenticated, requiring costly "fiscal stamps" for each document. There was a lot of "red tape" in Cameroon – probably a leftover from the French colonial system. Those documents, or certificates, are required for all government employment in Cameroon – and 90% of the jobs were government jobs. Without the correct documents and certificates, your employment could be delayed. I had difficulty getting my dossier papers in order because it seemed that the office workers and staff were never in their offices during regular business hours. And in addition, locating the correct offices was a challenge – for business addresses were non-existent. I was dependent on some "good Samaritan" accompanying me or someone giving me specific directions or relevant information, such as, "the Information & Culture building is across the street from Polygamy Bar." Of course, if I didn't know where Polygamy Bar was, the information was totally useless. It was all frustrating. My file had been lost once, so I had to put together another copy and buy additional stamps! This all took many days.

Arriving in Yaoundé from Kumba I should have known there would be many delays. Many folks had told me about all the documents to be verified and stamped and out-of-the-way government agencies to be visited. But I didn't believe it could be so difficult. After two weeks, I was given my own on-the-job personal office in the Ministry of Education building. Soon after settling into my new position, I went on maternity leave.

Government employees were provided with furnished housing – an unusual and generous benefit. I was convinced that the reason we secured a government apartment so soon was because I was nine months pregnant. Perhaps the officials at the Ministry of Education understood that I could not prepare for delivering my baby in the hotel where we had been staying. We felt very blessed, for many people didn't get housing for up to a year after they were employed.

The government flat was located in a pleasant area in Yaoundé called Tschinga. The residence was on the lower level, one of four similar units, all quite spacious. The brick structure was surrounded by an intricate wrought-iron fence and ornamented with gorgeous foliage. Inside the compound, the yard was beautifully and artistically terraced, -- with rock-lined footpaths. A large mango tree graced the backyard, and two smaller ones hung over the front balcony. The furnishings inside were more than adequate: two chairs and two couches – all wooden with caned seats and a small refrigerator and mini gas stove. The sitting room was approximately 25 feet by 25 feet! The entire floor area was covered with ceramic tile. To complement our large parlor, there was an open balcony facing the street, three bedrooms, a bathroom (complete with a bidet), a toilet room, a large kitchen, and a laundry room. Our apartment was truly luxurious – much nicer and definitely larger than anywhere we had lived in the U.S., remembering our former university housing and dumpy unit above the plumbing supply store.

But all the niceties could not redress our ailing relationship. My pregnancy diffused Christopher's temper somewhat, for he gloried in my being "with child." I had been protected from his temper and his moods when I was with his siblings in Kumba and Buea, but now I had no one to insulate me. It bothered Christopher that I obtained a government position before he did. Perhaps it hurt his pride. But whatever the case, Chris continued to treat me like a piece of his property, and I couldn't bear to be around him.

I spent many days in January walking up and down the streets of Tschinga, hoping to coax my body to go into labor, but perhaps I was still too anxious to deliver in new surroundings. My plan was to check into the Central Hospital in Yaoundé. Most non-Cameroonian women registered at one of many private clinics, but when I checked out those clinics, I discovered that the majority of the European doctors who practiced at them were quite inexperienced since they could not land jobs in their countries of origin. I therefore decided to go to the public hospital in the city where I would be able to employ a Cameroonian doctor. However, the normal procedure in Cameroon was to bring your own midwife to the hospital with you. Unless, of course, you wished to deliver your baby by yourself. It was not customary for Cameroonian doctors to deliver babies unless there were complications – breech births, for example.

I managed to find a Cameroonian doctor, but when I tried to make an appointment, I learned that appointments were non-existent and impossible. I had to go to the hospital and wait – for hours. Luckily, I arrived early that day. Fitemi and Bentasi accompanied me because Chris said he needed to go job hunting. We arrived at the corridor in front of the hospital around 9am or thereabouts. There were dozens of children playing around the corridor, and my kids had a lot of fun running and jumping about with the other children. What I was not prepared for was the long wait. I think I was there more than seven or eight hours. I was shocked at the number of people sitting on the benches and the stone walls outside – probably more than fifty, mostly women and children. We sat on one of ten or eleven long benches adjacent to the hospital. Finally, I saw the doctor. He checked me, and I was given the "all clear." I decided to not make another trip before I delivered.

Early in the morning on the 26th of January, I felt some labor pains. The electricity went out while I was showering! Christopher left to find a midwife. While driving to the hospital, during my acute labor contractions, Chris located a sixteen-year-old girl, Alice Taku, who agreed to accompany us. She climbed into our taxi and traveled to the hospital with us. Alice helped me get settled. She comforted me while I sat down on a very wobbly single bed, one of a dozen or so in that poorly lit hospital room. The mattress was bare—there was no bedding. Alice sent Chris home to fetch sheets, meds, towels, a nightgown, and some other needed supplies. Women were "camped out" with their own blankets and bedding all around the room; some sat on the floor alongside the walls, others rested under the beds – they were all there to help their mothers or sisters or aunties or friends because there were no nurses or attendants in the hospital. Each patient brought her own "staff." Some women were even set up to cook! Aromas of fufu and peanut soup were in the air.

I wondered why Chris had not informed me of all those customs. My doctor arrived a few hours later, and he predicted delivery would happen in about four hours. Then he left, not to return. When Alice and I were pretty sure I was ready, I got up out of bed and walked to that delivery room. No gurneys or wheel chairs in *l'Hopital Centrale*! The distance from the labor room to the delivery room seemed endless. I barely made it! There was no delivery bed – just a strange-looking chair that resembled a skeleton-like recliner. Sarikki was born seconds after I entered the delivery room – that "delivery chair" worked really well, adding help from gravity. My third delivery, but definitely the easiest and fastest one. I walked back to the labor room. Alice strolled beside me, joyfully carrying little Sarikki Klaaren Forgwe. I was looking forward to rest. I remember envisioning how tough and hardy Cameroonian women must be. Sarikki's arrival was a unique journey.

As I was dozing off, I overheard Alice asking Chris for the mosquito net. He didn't know he was supposed to bring one, and he told Alice he thought we didn't need one because his kid was strong and could fight off any disease. I slept. When I awoke, Sarikki was nowhere in sight!

Alice was frantic, exclaiming, "I'm sorry, Ma'am, sorry. They just couldn't help themselves!"

Not accustomed to having a non-native Cameroonian birthing her baby in *l'Hopital Centrale*, the Cameroonian mothers passed little Sarikki from bed to bed and from room to room throughout the entire place – just to get a good look at him. He was eventually delivered back to me contented and smiling. Alice and I became good friends. She stayed with me in the hospital, accompanied me home to Tschinga, and continued to regularly visit Sarikki and me at our flat. Alice was an angel – I'll never forget her.

My pregnancies had a calming effect on Christopher, the proud father. He was overjoyed to now have **two sons**. But after baby Sarikki entered the world, arrived home in Tschinga, and settled into life with his new family, Christopher's cheerful demeanor became quite supercilious. I felt a storm brewing beneath his pride and tranquility; Christopher's aggressive spirit came out of remission soon after my pregnancy ended. His old patterns returned.

Feeling drained and bone-tired from the childbirth and childcare of three children, my mood improved dramatically when my neighbor, Marie, dropped by one evening to invite me to see the film *"A Star Is Born."* Initially, I figured it would not be feasible for me to accept Marie's tempting invitation, but MaryAnn joyfully offered to take care of all three little Forgwes; MaryAnn strongly encouraged me to go out and enjoy myself at the movie. Marie and I took a taxi to the theater. We could hardly find a seat. The place was packed. Fortunately, we located some "space" between rows. Everyone was drinking beer and smoking -- quite a bizarre theater atmosphere; it was not at all what I was accustomed to. It was virtually impossible to hear anything – but since it was in French with English subtitles, the lack of audio didn't bother me! I adjusted to the system, and we had a great time.

My merriment ended, however, when I arrived home in Tschinga. Uncharacteristically, Christopher walked through our door at a very early hour that evening.

After discovering where I had been, he screamed, exclaiming, "Marie is an unsuitable and unfit person for you to attend a movie with; and, furthermore, your place is to always stay home with our children!"

As I walked across our sitting room, Chris punched me in the face, throwing me onto the floor. My nose bled for hours.

Yaoundé evenings were alive – kind of like county fairs when I was a child in Iowa. The warmth each day often acquiesced to a cooler temperature, and the city soon filled with people and activity. On rare occasions, I would open our iron gate and stroll down the local Tschinga streets. My senses were awakened by the pleasing aromas. Women from surrounding villages set up various shops nightly alongside the roadways in Yaoundé. Most merchants had shabby carts to move from place to place. I was unacquainted with most of the delicacies, but I tried them all. I threw myself into Cameroonian culture, craving to sample new, fresh experiences.

Open fire roasting, a natural and ancient way of preparing food, had in Cameroon been raised to a level of culinary artistry. Fish and chicken, available in abundance, were prepared over open fires and eaten with roasted or fried ripe plantains or potatoes. Locally made kettles were set up alongside the walkways, with meat and vegetables positioned on the grill directly over the coals. A gentle fire assured an evenly grilled juicy roast. Groups of friends sat 'round the prepared meal, eating together using their fingers. I remembered Mom's advice to never eat with my hands or fingers, but, nevertheless, I was now in a different place, and I enjoyed the food their way. Wines and beers and laughter smoothed down the feast.

Those roadway roasts were a well-established occurrence in Cameroon. A different choice from those chicken and fish roasts was the very popular "soya" – a beef barbecue much loved by all Cameroonians. A huge lump of meat was roasted on an open grill. While waiting for customers, dabs of seasoning sauces were spread and dribbled over the beef chunk in order to maintain its juiciness. Each vendor would chip bits of soya from the big lump according to the buyer's request. Onion, salt, garlic, pepper, more seasoning sauce, or spices could be further added. Not far from Tschinga there was an area called Briqueterie, which had assumed the name *"Ministry of Soya"* because of its tasty and popular soya treats. Bentasi and Fitemi loved the hot, spicy fish. There were few evenings they didn't beg me to buy some for them. Sugar cane was the only things that would console them if I couldn't find any fish. Whenever we bought treats, we carried our own containers. We would bring pieces of paper that could be rolled up in the shape of a cone. One of our favorite snacks was "koki," or bean cakes. Beans, of which several varieties were used, were soaked for a few hours and then briskly scrubbed to remove the skin. The grains were liquidized, and the resulting paste was vigorously stirred into a light pudding to which appropriate ingredients were added. Red palm oil was used to achieve a rich yellow color. The mixture was poured into a watertight banana leaf-spread, which was then folded and tied at the top. The "bundles" were steamed over gentle heat for two hours or more. The outcome was a yellow cake very pleasing to the palate. Eaten with plantains or cocoyams, koki was washed down with plenty of palm wine.

Egusi, prepared in nearly the same way as koki, came out a protein-rich white cake full of flavor. The oily paste was sometimes mixed with fish or meat to accentuate its food value. All those dishes were delicious – tastes and textures I had never before experienced! The cuisine could only be "topped" by the gracious and friendly folks who shared it together. Bentasi loved eating the coated-termites and grasshoppers.

Every neighborhood in Yaoundé had its own unique set of off-license bars. People enjoyed drinking their *"Brasserie Speciale," "Trente*

Trois," etc. – beers brewed and bottled in Cameroon. *"Bastos Minty"* cigarettes were commonplace. Palm wine was routine with most meals. When it was fresh, it was very sweet, but when it fermented, it became more potent than beer or wine.

Petty thievery was generally taken care of within seconds after an offense. Courts weren't needed for such minor misconducts. Anyone caught confiscating someone else's property was immediately mobbed by all witnesses in the area. The normal consequence was caning or thrashing by the crowd. Stealing and pilfering were rare.

A sincere feeling of caring permeated everyone's lives, with citizens taking responsibility for each other and the good of their community. People enjoyed life, even in the face of poverty. Cameroonians were generous people, never hesitating to share. Dance and art were inherent in all realms of existence. Stunning wood carvings and masks were delicately and artistically shaped. Many artisans displayed their wares at the markets and on the streets. Cameroon has produced many artists, particularly in music. Beginning in the 1970s with memorable pieces like Francis Bebey's *"Idiba"* and *"Kinshasa,"* the scene was set with *"Soul Makossa"* by Manu Debango, a famous Cameroonian musician. Cameroon has been recognized for its excellent football (known to Westerners as soccer), of which it continues to export home-grown players to Europe.

Occasionally, we attended Sunday mass in Nglonkok, where *bikutsi* dancers were featured in an "open air" service. One Sunday, the kids and I attended a service there with my friend, Josette. Worshipping in the fresh outdoors and being enthralled by the rhythm and the dancing was uplifting. I left Nglonkok overflowing with emotion and cheerfulness.

But the cheerfulness ended the following Monday evening. Arriving home from work, I prepared supper and spent time with my children; we ate and went for a walk around Tschinga. After the kids went to bed, I washed the dishes, picked up the little messes they had made, and soaked Sarikki's diapers. Then I sat at the dining room table and began writing some letters. It was a quiet evening – the kids and I were the only ones in the house. Around midnight, Chris came home. He walked through the front door straight into the bathroom. I greeted him, but he said nothing. Then he stepped into our bedroom. I heard a "clickety-click" noise of what sounded like Chris opening something – probably his combination-locked suitcase.

"Who's been fooling around with this lock?"

I froze. He stormed out of the bedroom and into the back washroom, shouting wild accusations. I heard a swish of water!

"Why aren't these diapers washed?"

Before I could elude his rage, he grabbed my arms and threw me against the wall. Yanking me up by my hair, he struck me across the back of my head. I don't remember much else – except that I was lying on the living room floor when the sun came up. Christopher was not there. I boiled some water for a warm bath and cleaned myself up. The blood quickly washed away, but the bruises remained.

Yaoundé was a city of contrasts. Large contemporary buildings rising above rows of crude shacks. Prosperous and destitute side by side. Modern air-conditioned grocery stores with plastic-wrapped meats and smelly, earthy country markets complete with chickens flying overhead. Hordes of yellow taxis and herds of cattle. Most environs had a unique blend of tropical foliage coupled with "never-picked-up" rubbish. The equatorial leafage was so stunning, however, that the image of garbage magically disappeared.

My life, too, was full of contrasts – fresh new experiences tarnished by reoccurring old patterns. But fortunately, I was surrounded by close friends and relatives. Fitemi, Bentasi, Sarikki, and I were often the center of attention. On many occasions, friends and relatives stayed with us, which was typical of Cameroonian culture. People around made me happy. I didn't want to be alone. I think a lot of my wanting others present was that it was less likely that Chris would lose his temper. However, Chris had a hard time adjusting to many of the idiosyncrasies of life in Cameroon. Friends and relatives often asked to borrow Christopher's tapes, books, and other paraphernalia from the U.S. Sharing was the

Cameroonian way. Chris was not comfortable lending out his things; he embraced the "individualism" he learned when living in the United States. He had forgotten or overlooked Cameroonian culture. Actually, I fit in better than he did.

My job with the Cameroonian government involved assisting University of Yaoundé students to obtain venues for continuing their education abroad. Most of the young people I worked with were from West Cameroon and were, therefore, fluent in English. They were all highly motivated. My office, in the main building of the Ministry of Education, was near Nglonkok. The government provided our housing, but the work compensation was very low and extremely slow in arriving. Cameroonians complained about the slow-paying government all the time. And Christopher let me know before my first day of work that I would not get a paycheck for a long time. Therefore, I looked and found some additional employment. I did some administrative and clerical work at the American Embassy, and I also obtained a position as an administrative assistant for a U.S.AID and U.S. Department of Agriculture joint venture called the "Sahel Food Crop Protection Project." Needless to say, I was very busy, but it was a good plan on my part to seek out other opportunities – for my first monies from my Cameroonian full-time position arrived after being on the job for an entire year! Without MaryAnn caring for her niece and nephews, I don't know how we would have survived. I worked ten to twelve hours a day, plus weekend and evening hours. I continued to be the main provider for our family. With three small children and three jobs, I was exhausted. But on the positive side, all those work contacts enabled me to delve into Cameroonian life and culture – and also helped me keep my distance from Christopher.

After more than a year in Cameroon, I had not yet met Christopher's parents, Mama and Papa Forgwe. Travel in Cameroon was complicated. Mama and Papa lived in Bamenda in the Northwest Province, quite a long trek from Yaoundé. And a year earlier, when Christopher, Fitemi, and Bentasi traveled to Bamenda, I was unable to traverse the bumpy roads and hazardous conditions because of my pregnant state. I longed to meet Christopher's parents, but because of Cameroon's lack of in-country communications and the expense of traveling, I was unsure when that would happen.

Surprisingly, my mom and dad came to Yaoundé when Rikki was nine months old – before Christopher's parents had been able to make the trip. We did lots of sightseeing and touring during their visit. Dad, who had a truly adventuresome spirit, had a fantastic time. He was really in his element; walking all around the city, conversing with many folks, and sampling a lot of the goodies. Mom enjoyed herself, too -- playing with her grandchildren and getting acquainted with MaryAnn. But the array of insects and lizards made her quite squeamish! Mom and Dad's visit was a happy time for me and the kids. I thought about talking to my parents honestly about how everything for me was really going pretty poorly, but I could not end my silence and reveal to them the many ways Christopher was abusing me – just as I never told anyone about Chicago. I wondered what was keeping me from speaking my mind.

Christopher behaved himself temporarily – until one weekend when he and I attended a friend's wedding. My parents and MaryAnn stayed home with the children. After the wedding ceremony, Chris told me he had been asked to photograph the wedding party. He loved his photographic exploits, so I was complicit when he suggested I go home ahead of him while he remained to take pictures.

And when I arrived back in Tschinga, I found Mama and Papa Forgwe in our apartment! Wow! What a pleasant surprise. It was our first meeting. I was overjoyed to welcome them and pleased Christopher's parents and my parents could get acquainted. What a special and unusual happening! They were all talking and laughing as I adjusted to the marvelous surprise. Mama and Papa Forgwe were very outgoing and friendly. Mama Martina squeezed me robustly, radiating a genuine welcoming tone. She was youthful for having mothered six children! It was apparent that Mama was the queen of the family. Papa Matthias was quite tall, standing at least a full inch above his eldest son, Christopher. He and I hugged enthusiastically. Papa was kind and pleasant, drawing everyone into the activities at hand. We all got acquainted and conversed and laughed far into the early morning hours. But I wondered when Christopher would return. My dad snapped photos of everyone in the family, and he also photographed our beautiful apartment and yard. We finally all retired to our bedrooms for restful sleep.

My sleep was not restful. Christopher never came home that night. The instant Mama Forgwe realized her son had not returned until the morning, she became very annoyed and angry. She was livid that Christopher had not been a dutiful husband and father and come back to his wife and his children, not to mention his wife's visiting parents. Mama followed Chris around all day, lecturing him non-stop in both Meta, her native language, and Pidgin English. Papa also participated in the quashing of Christopher's behavior, but Mama Martina ran the show. Christopher's parents were now at least somewhat aware of their son's waywardness. I was humiliated and hurt by Christopher's actions and behavior. But it was nothing new.

My parents left the following week. Again, I debated telling them about Christopher's abusiveness, but I guess I was not ready. I was certain Mom and Dad sensed not much had changed. After all, they witnessed the same scenarios that we all did.

Home mailboxes did not exist in 1970s Cameroon. Houses were not numbered. You were lucky to be on a street with a name. Therefore, mail was delivered to offices, churches, institutions, etc. – not to residences. When we first arrived in Yaoundé we asked Paul, one of Christopher's cousins, to receive our mail; Paul was employed with the Post Office, so it seemed convenient. When I began my employment with the Ministry of Education, we had our own address, so our mail was delivered to me at work. I was confused the morning a young man dropped off, at my office, a bundle of mail addressed to *"Christopher Forgwe, in care of Mr. Muna, Head of the General Assembly."* The young messenger said that since he was so close to my office that morning, it was more convenient to deliver the letters to me instead of to Christopher, which was his usual procedure. I could see that my husband was keeping his mail a secret!

As I sorted through that mail, I saw a letter from Zeeland, Michigan, from Yolanda to Chris! I couldn't prevent myself from reading the letter. The first line, *"To the King of Fire,"* and the last line, *"From Your Queen of Hearts,"* sandwiched many pages of remembrances of past intimate moments and longings for each other.

I looked at my life and wondered why. I felt used. I was scared. I was hurt. I was angry. I avoided any intimacy with my husband. I went to bed before he came home and jumped out of bed early in the morning before he opened his eyes. The avoidance pattern went on for months. And then, one night in January, Chris was in an unusually amorous mood. He arrived home uncharacteristically early. I had not yet retired, for the kids were still playing. When I looked at how he acted, I began to get fearful. The kids fell asleep, and he sat down next to me on the couch. Christopher stroked my hair and wrapped his arm around me. He demanded that I come to bed, but when he noticed my lack of interest, he firmly grabbed my left arm. As I tried to release myself from his grip, he yanked me toward him, twisting my nose.

I said "NO," but it didn't matter.

Christopher continued to have difficulty finding a job. While I was working and MaryAnn tended Fitemi, Bentasi, and Sarikki, Christopher searched for employment in-between partying, visiting friends, and pursuing his photography hobby. After many months, Chris found a job — but his starting date was to be announced later; however, the day after Chris was informed of his employment, he reported to his worksite for training. On that very day, I was so nauseated that I decided to stay home from work. What could be happening? I thought about it, and I surmised that I was experiencing some "morning sickness" symptoms. I knew it. I was pregnant! I could not believe it. How would I handle all of this? And to make it worse, despite my work schedule, Chris continued to demand that I do most of the domestic around-the-house chores.

I carried on, but I was in a daze. I went to my work sites the next day, but when I arrived home, I found Christopher distraught that I had not laundered his clothes. He indicated he would need clean clothing for his job training. He pushed me onto the floor in the laundry room, and when I tried to stand up, he slapped me across the mouth. Bentasi started crying, and Chris left the house. MaryAnn helped me wash the clothes, but she refused to speak to her brother for about a two-week period. MaryAnn and I spent a lot of time together. She wanted to enroll at the University of Yaoundé. I assisted with her school fees, and she moved in with us in Tschinga. MaryAnn helped me around the house and with the kids. She shared with me her perceptions about life in Cameroon. She taught me how to make chin-chin, Cameroonian cookies. I taught her how to play "Euchre," "Pounce," and "Scrabble." She told me how hard Cameroonian women labored in the fields and what they had to endure. MaryAnn had so much energy, and she was always cheerful. The kids adored her. She begged me to tell her stories about the U.S. We became very close. But I didn't share everything. I tried to hide the turmoil between Christopher and me. I wasn't always successful, however. There was no way she didn't see what was going on with the relationship between me and her brother.

Primus, Christopher's brother, was an aspiring actor. He belonged to an acting group called the *"Buea Performing Troupe."* When they performed in Yaoundé, I looked forward to attending and witnessing him and his troupe in action. The night of their first performance I got ready to go, but Chris forbade me to leave the house. He said that Cameroonian women were expected to stay home with their children. Primus found out about that weeks later. A rift developed between the brothers, which I think did not mend for years.

I entertained the hope of leaving Christopher. Knowing it was not feasible, I began to despair. It seemed as if I was in prison. Chris was becoming more and more aware of my unhappiness; I knew he would never allow me and the kids to fly to Michigan to visit my parents. I was sure, however, that he would permit me to go by myself.

At some point, I made a conscious change in attitude. I made an effort to appear happy if only to open a small window of possibility for a chance to abscond. I hid my fatigue and never divulged how nauseous

I felt during my fourth pregnancy. I worked as cheerfully as possible, grabbing onto all the opportunities for enjoyment that presented themselves.

When I discovered it would be possible to visit Njindom, however, I was sincerely happy. I didn't have to pretend. My sweetest Cameroonian memories are of Njindom, Mama and Papa Forgwe's village home in the Northwest Province. For more than a year, I eagerly anticipated the journey to Bamenda. I unwillingly stayed behind when Christopher, Fitemi, and Bentasi traveled to Njindom late in 1977, when I was too pregnant to traverse the rocky back roads.

A year after Sarikki was born, our entire family – all five of us – piled into my dilapidated Volkswagen van and drove to Bamenda. Except for the paved highway from Douala to Victoria, the roadways were single-laned and dirt or gravel-covered, and many of them too narrow to accommodate more than one vehicle at a time. A late start prevented us from arriving at the first ferry on time, so we spent the night near a riverbank at the mercy of the mosquitoes. The next day, the van broke down high in Baffousam's rolling foothills. Chris and I maneuvered the van off a hilly, narrow road; we slept inside, serenaded by the soothing night sounds of the grasslands. Chris summoned a bush taxi.

At daybreak, we arrived in the area called Bamenda. The scenery was breathtaking. I had never seen such lush countryside – green waving grasses, cool fresh waterfalls, and so much succulent foliage. Njindom was simple and quiet – undisturbed by any modern-day amenities. Cool brick and stone houses with neatly thatched roofs were arranged in sets of compounds. In Njindom, Meta was the spoken language, and it went back centuries.

Christopher's parents were gracious and accommodating. Villagers from miles around Mbengwi Division came to greet me and my husband and our three children. A big arrival event was planned. Young boys delivered gourds of palm wine into Mama and Papa's compound. I loved the palm wine. It was sweet and flavorful; I recalled the many gourds of wine delivered to my home in Tschinga when Sarikki was born.

Lots of goats were slaughtered and prepared for dining. We feasted on a variety of Cameroonian foods. Mama prepared several baskets of pounded cocoyams and boiled plantains to be eaten with delicious African peanut stew. Over an open fire, she made a hearty brew with collard greens, dried meat, and kola nuts – while Bentasi and Fitemi assisted her by blowing on the hot embers. The villagers prepared and contributed dishes from "egusi" to "achu." Corn fufu was arranged on banana leaves and eaten with a rich and spicy-type goulash made with okra. As the fufu dishes were passed, each male guest picked up a portion with his first two fingers and his thumb, dipping it into the hearty stew. Then the fufu and stew combo was swallowed – not chewed. Women and children were typically served after the men-folks. However, being the number one guest at that event, I was invited to eat first.

After devouring the many edibles, we sang and danced. Some young villagers fastened on anklets of kola kernels, which clashed as they moved. We clapped to the rhythm of tall drums, mesmerized by the palm wine, the music, and the grassland night air. We spent the evening drinking from calabashes of fresh palm wine, talking, laughing, and dancing – all by the light of kerosene lamps, casting shadows on people's faces.

Life in Njindom was, for me, like relaxing on an old-fashioned camping trip in another place and time. No electricity. No running water. Everything natural. Nights and days competed equally for length. On my first day in Njindom, twelve full hours of brightness yielded sharply to total darkness. And I mean total darkness! MaryAnn lit matches for me as we strolled and giggled in complete darkness. It was magical, something I had never ever experienced.

I woke up the next morning to find the kids playing. Christopher was nowhere around. Many Njindom folks asked me about where my husband was, but I had to answer honestly that I did not know. I enjoyed my visit in Njindom immensely, probably because my husband was not around much – and when he was, his family insulated me from him. But I had difficulty understanding his lack of respect for his parents, not to mention his lack of respect and consideration for me.

As the sun came up, Papa Forgwe was down at the riverbank helping Fitemi and Bentasi explore. Mama was bathing Sarikki in her tin washtub. Three young Forgwe cousins walked down to the river to draw water for Rikki's bath. I walked out back to shower. Papa filled two large barrels with fresh water. He neatly set out some unusual-looking bar soap and a stiff linen-type towel. The shower was a small cubicle, much like a "lean-to" back on those Iowa farms in the '50's. The water buckets were strategically positioned to let as much or as little cool water stream down my body as desired. I felt refreshed.

I dressed for the day, and Fitemi and Bentasi came running back from the riverbank, telling tales of pigs and goats and snakes. Then, they left with Grandma to check out her groundnut farm. Sarikki and I, freshly bathed, basked in the sunlight. When Temi and Tasi returned, they carried baskets of fresh groundnuts and potatoes.

I wondered why and where Christopher had disappeared to, but I didn't let his absence and rudeness spoil my day. Actually, it was more enjoyable for me with his absence. I tried to help with the daily chores around the Forgwe compound and in Njindom, but I wasn't allowed to do much. Everyone insisted on waiting on me and the kids. It was a refreshing change from my life in our Tschinga flat back in Yaoundé.

I talked a lot with Christopher's dad; we shared many great stories and experiences – some told by me about my Iowa roots and others humorously relayed by Papa Matthias, from a long life growing up in the cool grasslands of Bamenda. We both smiled and chuckled a lot that day. I wanted to speak more with Mama, but I needed an interpreter -- for she spoke only Meta and Pidgin English. Fortunately, my sister MaryAnn cheerfully accommodated us, and Mama Martina and I got to know each other a lot better. The hours were spent sharing and enjoying one another's company. It was a relaxing time, sipping on palm wine and nibbling on fresh mangoes and papaya.

Daylight, again, ended abruptly. But on my second day in Njindom, nightfall was different than the first -- the evening sky was brilliant with moonlight. When the stars appeared, they shimmered in what looked like a huge black dome. The earth was peaceful. My visit to Njindom was a magical dream. The people were remarkable – very kind and generous and gracious.

After two days, Christopher returned to the village with no explanation of his whereabouts! He reproached me for questioning him. It seemed like he was trying hard to blemish my Cameroon experiences. He roamed when and where he desired, never respecting me enough to communicate his activities. When he was near me, he was usually "on my back," directing me, commanding me, "Do this, do that," ordering me around. Christopher was possessed.

There were times I feared for my safety.

CHAPTER 5

Endings

Bamenda was heavenly – I was happy and carefree there with Mama and Papa Forgwe, laughing and hanging out – protected from Christopher's outbursts of temper. But now it was time to return to work and school.

It seemed strange that the presence of Christopher's family did not deter his disappearances. I wondered why Chris would choose to miss such festive gatherings. Fitemi, Bentasi, and Sarikki were the center of all those celebrations, but Christopher continued to leave us alone and stranded, wondering where he had gone off to.

Those wonderful memories of life in Njindom and the Mbwengi region can never be duplicated. I will keep them in my heart and mind forever, as everyone donned colorful and festive batiks and other stunning garments. All the Forgwe family folks and dozens of Njindom villagers celebrated our homecoming to their village home with dancing and music.

Such great memories. Fitemi and Bentasi's faces had beamed in the bright moonlight as everyone from kilometers around whirled 'round and 'round in a huge circle – surrounding a crackling fire. We had enjoyed stomping to rhythmic music and dancing robustly, bikutsi-style. Young Njindom villagers played bata and djembe drums. I soaked in those moments, for nothing in my experience had ever equaled it. The visit was a welcome relief from my circumstances, as the music beat through each night we were there.

But now we were returning home, fortunate that Cousin Paul offered to drive us back to Yaoundé. I would have liked to stay in Bamenda longer, but work responsibilities were waiting. I gazed out at the ravishing countryside – dotted with waving raffia palms tucked randomly in and out of the sunken valleys and depressions. Fitemi told me Grandma called Bamenda the "grassfields."

As we motored through the grasslands, we passed through the area where my VW van had broken down on our way to Njindom a week earlier. Drawing closer to Baffousam, I wondered about the condition of my broken-down, rusty old van that never made it to Mama and Papa's place. The van's tie rod was cracked, and it seemed repairs would be impossible. And we had barely made it past the mosquito-infested river ferry. It had been impossible to get any help – no communication, no phones, no service garages, no electricity, no way to see anything in complete darkness! We had to sleep in my van that night – at the mercy of the mosquitoes! Would I ever retrieve my VW? I didn't think so. I prayed we would not have any vehicle delays on our drive back to Yaoundé. I wondered how I would get to and from work without my van. Passing near Baffousam, I peeked out the window and wondered if my VW could possibly be resting among those palm trees alongside the roadway. Or was it hiding amongst the smaller Raphia, the palms with subterranean stems – roots which could camouflage my auto-bus? Everything was deliciously green as the leaves rose up from the ground, forming funnel-like crowns – with shaggy hanging leaflets. I speculated my van was gone forever.

Fitemi slept in the back seat of Paul's car; she was propped up on that scratchy gunny sack packed full of Grandma Forgwe's potatoes and nuts

– sent from her garden and groundnut farm. I slipped one of Sarikki's soft, dry diapers under Temi's head to soften the "potatoes" and wipe off the sweat dripping down her cheeks. Bentasi peered out the window, looking for lizards and insects and perhaps even some screeching red or green monkeys.

As we straddled those bumpy roads back to Yaoundé, I feared the return of Christopher's unpredictable temper. I envisioned leaving him – but I knew it would take a miracle to pull it off. Now that I was ready to leave him, it seemed that it was impossible.

Back in Yaoundé, it was time for me to return to work and for Fitemi and Bentasi to return to school. My husband would be beginning his new-found employment soon. He had only recently received word that he had a position. Perhaps he should have finished his anthropology degree while we were still in Michigan. I never did find out exactly why we left so quickly to return to Cameroon – and why he never finished his Ph.D.! It had been almost two years since Christopher had been employed.

My mini-vacation was over, and I was returning to work. I enjoyed working at the Education Ministry, for there was cooperation and trust among my co-workers. The students I counseled were very appreciative of the resources and services I was able to provide for them – programs available to fund their educational goals and advice on possible institutions where there were possibilities for study abroad. A little ironic since I secretly also wanted to go abroad!

Securing that Cameroonian government position provided my family with our beautiful and spacious apartment in Tschinga. Where would we have lived if I had not landed that job at the Ministry of Education?

My other jobs, obtained through the American Embassy and US-A.I.D., were part-time, but they were necessary to pay for school fees for Temi and Tasi. I worked mornings and early afternoons at the Ministry of Education; and late afternoons, evenings, and some weekends doing various administrative jobs at the American Embassy or as an administrative assistant for a project at U.S. AID. All those work environs enabled me to function and for my family to be supported.

All of the people I interacted with through work projects and responsibilities – from Cameroon, the U.S., and many countries around the globe – made me appreciate what I had and appreciate the vast and diverse culture of Cameroon.

But at the end of each work day, I returned to many household duties. My evenings were always spent with my children and were the highlight of each and every day. But much too often, those happy times were under a shadow – the shadow of Christopher's temper.

One rainy evening, soon after returning from Njindom, my friend picked me up to go to the Briqueterie market. Bentasi came running out to Esther's car, exclaiming: "Auntie Esther, Auntie Esther! Guess what? Daddy didn't give Mommy a bloody nose today!"

Esther and I were dumbfounded. Christopher's violence had always been directed at me, and me alone; but his violence was not escaping my children! Bentasi's words rang in my ears – making clear to me that Christopher's treatment of me had repercussions on Fitemi, Bentasi, and Sarikki. I could see that Bentasi had come to accept his father's abuse of me as a normal and regular occurrence. Bentasi was very happy that day when nothing bad happened to his mom – and he wanted to share his happiness with Auntie Esther.

At some point, I had enough. It's hard to say when that was, exactly, for I was in a fog. But I remember beginning to plan my escape from my husband the night Donatus Ngono, our next-door neighbor, was visiting us.

I was preparing dinner when Christopher yelled from the living room, "Joy, where did you put my acrylics?"

When I answered that I had not seen his paints, he proceeded to call me names, demeaning me for not knowing the location of his art supplies.

With a friend present, I was humiliated and embarrassed. Christopher continued to ridicule me, so I slowly moved toward the parlor entrance door. He grabbed me and ripped off my dress. Then he tore it in half! Fitemi and Bentasi began crying, and they begged him to stop. Donatus pulled Christopher off me and tried to calm him down.

From within Donatus' grip, Chris shrieked, "Go ahead and leave if you want to! Go out that door! Go back to Michigan. But **my** children will **never** leave Cameroonian soil!"

I was nauseated by Christopher, but I carried out my "wifely duties" – for I had a plan – and the end was more important than the means. I planned to scheme out a strategy, act like nothing was amiss, and when the time was right, I would pick myself up and walk out that door, never to return – but not without all my children.

Where would I get support? For fear of discovery, I dared not share my plan with anyone. The American Embassy could not help me because the laws in Cameroon were very patrilineal – my husband's citizenship dictated mine. Cameroonian law prevented me from leaving the country without my husband's consent – even though I was an American citizen.

And what about Sarikki? He was little more than a year old. I had no access to his birth records. Why hadn't Chris declared Sarikki's birth and obtained a birth certificate? I would be traveling with three children while pregnant with my fourth. Time and effort to plan a workable escape plan had to be sandwiched between my work responsibilities. Not to mention children and household duties and activities. OMG! It was overwhelming.

And when I thought about Christopher's relationship with our children, I had second thoughts. He was very fond of them and loved them a lot. But not enough to help at home with their care! Christopher was not helping me by his daily activities – which were always involved in his pleasure and enjoyment. It was only recently that he had found employment. Christopher generally used his time for his own gratification.

As I carried out my work responsibilities and household chores, I felt trapped. I was living in fear and uncertainty, not knowing how to develop a plan to alleviate my circumstances. I did my best to function, which meant working hard at not irritating Christopher. My plan was in my head in many different versions, but I was going to make sure it happened. I would shut the door on my life with Christopher and never look back. I didn't care how futile it seemed – I would find a way, and I poured all my energy into exploring all the possibilities. I was not going to put up with any more from Chris – but I swore I would never leave without my children.

Securing the needed funds was the easiest part. My American friend, who worked as a physical therapist in Yaoundé, loaned me the necessary money – the equivalent of about $2,000. She only asked that I return the money to her bank account in Massachusetts after I arrived back in the U.S. I was eternally grateful.

I made an appointment with the American Ambassador and the First Secretary at the U.S. Embassy. I knew there would be roadblocks because I was aware that I needed my husband's consent to get an exit visa, but I hoped that even with the unfair laws in Cameroon, the American Embassy officials could do something – perhaps perform a miracle. After all, I was an American citizen. I soon discovered that my knowledge of the situation was correct – the embassy could not provide me with the needed visa. Damn that Cameroonian patrilineal shit. The visa issue was a huge obstacle.

I became aware that I had to leave illegally, as far as Cameroon law was concerned. The ambassador suggested that I have a fake passport made up just in case my point of departure from Cameroon required some collateral. Trusting I could find a way across the border in some unpopulated spot, I decided to take the ambassador's advice.

But arranging for the counterfeit passport would have to wait until ALL my children were listed on my passport! Fitemi and Bentasi were included on my passport, but Sarikki was not. I was NOT going to leave Sarikki in Cameroon. The ambassador suggested I do so – for my own safety. She felt a speedy departure was the wisest option. I did not feel the same way. Leaving without Rikki was never a possibility for me!

Christopher had never recorded Sarikki's birth! How was I going to get Sarikki on my passport without a birth certificate? I asked myself why Christopher did not declare his son's birth. Was it procrastination? I did not think so. The reason now was clear to me. Without a birth certificate, including Sarikki on my passport was impossible. That's just what he wanted.

I don't know where my fortitude came from, but I would not give up. I went to Yaoundé's City Hall, the government building where birth certificates and other licenses were issued. I hoped to obtain a document verifying Sarikki's birth in Cameroon. Not understanding English, the young Cameroonian clerk asked to speak to my husband. OMG!

I went back home to Tschinga, feeling very irritated and hopeless. Since my French was weak, I asked my good friend, Marie Bah, to help me. Marie was an American who was fluent in French. She accompanied me downtown the second week in February. She did the talking and explaining and pleading, but none of her efforts got us anywhere. We did not give up; we figured that if we pestered the city hall officials every day, someone would eventually get tired of us and produce the needed certificate. A trip to downtown Yaoundé became part of our daily routine. It was difficult to fit those treks in between work hours and home duties. Two months passed – and still no results. Daily returning home to Tschinga empty-handed was disheartening. And lying to Chris about my whereabouts drained my stamina. Marie and I worried that Christopher would discover what we were up to.

By April, Mabel Smythe, the U.S. Ambassador to Cameroon, advised me – for the second time – to leave Cameroon without Sarikki. Again, I did not consider her advice. It was unthinkable.

In May, success came with the help of a bribe. A young entry-level clerk produced the birth certificate when I slipped 50,000 francs CFA (a little less than $100) into his pocket. Rushing down to an out-of-the-way photoshop, I secretly had Sarikki's picture taken. With his birth certificate and photo in hand, I went to the U.S. Embassy and completed Sarikki's "report of an American birth abroad" papers. The embassy amended my passport to include my youngest son. There were many delays with my plan. A spirit of survival helped me put on a false front of contentment for Christopher's benefit. A spirit of survival veiled my fear and exhaustion.

In May of 1979, I wrote a letter to my parents. For speed and safety, I mailed it via the American Embassy.

"May 1, 1979

Dear Mom and Dad,

This letter I have been putting off writing for a long time. I've debated calling you, but there is so much I have to say, and you would have so many questions that I decided I should write first.

Well, I better get right to the point. First of all, I am pregnant again – this happened around the middle of January, so now I'm about 4 months. I pretty much accepted the fact when I first discovered it, but developments between Chris and me from January onwards have made this pregnancy only complicate our problems.

To make a long story short, Christopher's behavior the last 6 months has made me come to a very important decision – I really can't stay here with him. I thought that his coming back to Cameroon would calm him down – I thought that what he needed was to be in his own country so he could work and support his family instead of always depending on me.

Now, listen very closely. I have finally come to the realization that he has no intention of ever supporting us. I'm not saying that he won't work, for he is working now, but I'm convinced that I'm always going to be the one who works more and the one who really "carries the ball." I suppose this could be lived with if he respected me for doing this, but now (more than ever before) he is being very disrespectful of me as a wife, mother, and a human being. Let me give you some examples:

I came home from working one Sunday morning (from 7 till 1). I was working overtime, and I was very tired. The minute I walked in the door, Chris told me I should do some work in the house for a change, and he ordered me to immediately wash the diapers. I told him I wanted to sit down and rest a few minutes first. He told me there was work to do, and he then hit me across the face, almost breaking my nose. I lost a lot of blood, and I felt sick for days. When I told him he was acting crazy, he hit me again across the back of the head and in the stomach (and remember, I'm pregnant). Fitemi and, Bentasi, and Sarikki were all crying, not knowing what to think.

Another time, he started insulting me in front of Donatus (our neighbor). When I got up to leave, he tore my dress in half. Again, the children witnessed this. Donatus was very upset and tried to calm him down. The children were confused.

There are many other incidents, but I think I've told you enough. This kind of thing (the violence) had happened in the U.S. also, and I told him if it ever happened again, I would leave him. Of course, since he's been doing it here, he's been telling me the children are Cameroonians now, and they will never leave Cameroon.

Well, I think I have told you enough. What it all comes down to is that I'm upset, the children are upset and I am looking into the possibilities of coming back to the States. Of course I realize it is going to be very difficult for me alone in the States, but it can't be anything like I'm going through here. There is only so much I can stand. And I'm very tired. I'm working practically 7 days and nights a week. Also, Chris still corresponds regularly with Yolanda (which he doesn't know I know). As far as I'm concerned, it's all over for Christopher and me. But I will never leave here without my children. So, now that you know all the facts, I'm going to tell you my plans. You are not to discuss this with anyone. Don't write his parents or my friends here because if any Cameroonian finds out I want to leave, it will spoil my chances, and there will be nothing I can do, you can do, or the whole U.S. gov't can do to get me out of Cameroon.

First of all, I want you to know that I'm okay. Chris is still treating me badly, but I'm rolling with the punches and "pretending" to be very content. My plan is to make him think nothing is wrong, and when I get my chance, I'll leave.

Second, some friends are helping me, including the American Embassy. They all want me to leave as quickly and quietly as possible.

I plan to leave by way of North Cameroon. My passport is in order. I have declared Sarikki a U.S. citizen and amended my passport to include him. The problem is this: I cannot obtain an exit visa without Christopher's signature. Therefore, I cannot go to the airport and fly out because they will ask for an exit visa. But there are other ways. I have some friends in North Cameroon (U.S.AID employees) who have agreed to help me get across the border by car. They say there is no problem — people go back and forth all the time. So, as soon as I have the opportunity (when Chris is gone for a few days), I will leave. I will fly from Yaoundé to Maroua (in North Cameroon). Then my friends will drive me to either Chad or Nigeria (only a few hours' drive). Then I will fly to New York. The Embassy here can give me the necessary visas to be in either Chad or Nigeria.

The other problem is money — I don't have enough. I'm going to have to ask you for the necessary ticket money. I don't know how much it will be, but I have a friend here who wants to loan me the money, and then when I get back to the States, I can put the money (in dollars) in her account.

So, please don't worry, and don't write anything about this to me in a letter, because you never know who opens the mail here. (That's why I didn't send this letter in the international mail). I'll try to telephone you after you've had enough time to receive and read this letter.

Please share this with Mary Ann, Gene, and Keith. I will fly to New York and call Gene to pick me up there, so I want him to know what's going on.

Love, Joy

May 2

IMPORTANT. I just found out that my friend doesn't have quite enough money to loan me — it's costing more than I estimated. So, I need $700 (seven hundred dollars) minimum immediately.

This is how you must do it.

Telephone to: (Bureau of Consular Affairs) Welfare and Whereabouts, (202) 632-5225, Department of State, Washington, D.C.

Request that they establish a Trust Fund Account for daughter: Joy Forgwe in Yaoundé, Cameroon, in amount of $700.00.

You must find the quickest way to get the money to Washington (perhaps you can have the bank wire it).

Also, request (VERY IMPORTANT) that the Department cable an IMMEDIATE order to pay to the American Embassy, Yaoundé."

When I read over that letter, my body felt chilled. I never told Mom and Dad how hard I had been working and scheming and plotting for the last three months! I never told them about all the obstacles I had encountered before I posted their letter. I failed to mention how difficult it had been to include Sarikki on my passport. I didn't want them to worry.

After posting the letter, I arranged a meeting with the Vice Consul at the American Embassy. We discussed escape routes. Nigeria was the most plausible. The VC felt that leaving through Nigeria, an English-speaking country, would be less complicated for me. Exit through Chad would be dangerous, for Chad was in the middle of a civil war!

I decided to go along with the Vice Consul's advice, and pass through Nigeria, specifically Kano. It seemed like my plan was finally coming together. I received the money from my friend, and my parents sent more funds than I had asked for. Sarikki was listed on my passport. I was all set.

The next time I met with the Vice Consul, she gave me the name of a secretary at the Nigerian Embassy who would be able to arrange for my exit from Cameroon and my entry visa into Nigeria. Once in Nigeria, the American Embassy there would hopefully be able to handle the remaining paperwork. The VC offered to make an appointment for me to meet with the Nigerian secretary, but I declined, saying I would schedule it myself.

While relaxing in our parlor the evening after my meeting with the Vice Consul, I glanced over at the end table and saw an unfamiliar book – A Dance of the Forests, by Wole Soyinka. The cover had a grayish background with a spindly old man holding up a club in his right hand – and blowing into his raised-up other hand. I was curious and picked it up to take a closer look. Inside the book's cover, Christopher's name was written in a light blue ink. Skimming through the pages I saw Christopher's name again, in the same blue hue, written inside the back cover. But there was more than his name there. Jumping out of the page at me was an intimate inscription revealing the book was a "special" gift for Chris. As I gazed at the inscription's signature, my mouth fell open in disbelief. The book was given to my husband by the secretary at the Nigerian Embassy! What? How could that be? I scrutinized the book closely and uncovered a piece of ivory-colored parchment paper tucked between two pages. The paper crackled as I meticulously unfolded it very carefully to avoid ripping or damaging the note and causing suspicion of my tampering. I looked into the kitchen, and then toward the bathrooms and bedrooms – checking to make sure no one saw me there in the parlor. I inquisitively read the note. It said many things, but I failed to remember the specific words. The words were private and intimate – revealing a budding relationship! I quickly but carefully placed that book back – as if no one's eyes had fallen on it – on the top of that web-like end table.

Was some higher power assisting me? It must have been fate that I picked up that Soyinka book. If I had asked that Nigerian woman for help with my entry into Nigeria, Christopher surely would have discovered my plan. I had no choice but to exit through Chad – which meant crossing the crocodile-infested Chari River and traversing a war zone. The civil war in Chad, which began in the mid-1960s, was still ongoing.

And Chad would be my departure point? Anxiety smothered me. There were so many hurdles to overcome. I began to doubt myself and my plan. What if I got caught? What about the danger? I focused on my goal, trusting the details would fall into place. If I did not leave quickly, I would have to deal with yet another birth certificate problem.

I organized a party for Bentasi's fifth birthday, thinking a celebration would lend an aura of normalcy to our family life – with no hint of my departure plans. My friend Esther proposed to host Tasi's birthday party. Esther was an American; and she, like me, was married to a Cameroonian. Esther was one of the few people aware of my exit plan.

Around noon, May 15th, Fitemi, Bentasi, Sarikki, Christopher, and I took a taxi to Esther and Simon's apartment, which was in a complex called Cité Verte – Green City. Cité Verte was a residential compound built on the Messa hill. It was a composite of identical buildings separated and made of concrete with the exteriors usually of stucco. The one or two-story flats were lovely villas and the perfect location for a birthday party. The festivity made me feel crafty and devious as I watched Christopher gleefully snap photos of his eldest son.

When we arrived back in Tschinga after Bentasi's party, my kids giggled as they climbed into their beds for the night. Christopher retired early, without his usual disappearing routine – for he was enthused about journeying to Bamenda in the morning. None of my family had any hint of my following day's exodus.

Lying next to Christopher for the last time, I thought through the morning's details over and over. I had arranged for John, my supervisor at U.S.AID, to drive Christopher to the Northwest Province. But I did not inform John about my intentions. My husband would be going home, strategically and deceptively arranged by me, to spend time with his Mama and Papa in Njindom.

Christopher would be enjoying himself with his fellow Bamenda folks – many merry cousins, lively beautiful nieces, princely uncles; batik-adorned aunties, and probably a few striking young women sporting sleek Karite-drenched hairstyles, accompanied by their doting consorts.

Yes, he would be enjoying himself in Njindom, but he would soon be returning to Yaoundé—and Christopher would not find his family at home there in Tschinga. Perhaps, then, he would realize that his despicable behaviors and actions forced his wife to leave him.

Around 5:00 a.m. Christopher woke up. Peeking out from under the bed covers, I nervously watched him amble into the first bathroom – the very narrow one, slightly more than a meter and a half wide – furnished with only a miniature toilet and the tiniest sink ever made. I watched the wall geckos feasting on their morning breakfast – mosquitoes – just outside in the hallway.

Then I observed Christopher enter Bathroom Number Two, the spacious one – complete with a white stand-alone cast iron bathtub positioned on four pig-like feet, a shower dwarfed by a rarely used mini-hot-water heater, a very large washing sink, and, of course, a bidet, a leftover from the era of French colonialism. It was an elegant bathing room, with the exception of the flying cockroaches, of course. I watched the roaches, too – showing off their oval bodies and threadlike antennae. The cockroaches were flat-bodied, with feathery wings – and their leathery integuments shone brightly.

Those things I noticed because I was not planning to see them again, and I wanted to remember them. When I heard the water running, I rolled out from under the sheets and walked into the kitchen to brew some coffee. Esther had given me one of those French pots, crafted to work like an old percolator. I put in the grounds and water and placed the pot on my small gas stove.

John Franklin, an American businessman who was my boss at US AID, knocked at the front door; I opened it to let him in, and we greeted each other. John entered the parlor, and I noticed that his eyebrows were tightly furrowed as he started to ask why I was not going to Njindom with my husband. I raised my finger, and John decided to say nothing. He and I then briefly discussed an issue concerning the venture we were working on for the *"Sahel Food Crop Protection Project,"* in Mauritania.

Christopher entered the parlor carrying his leather alligator-like suitcase. He greeted John with a pleasant *"Bonjour."* I handed Christopher a generous number of francs CFA for his hiatus home. He took the money but did not thank me. John and Christopher walked out the door on their way to Njindom – a long and bumpy trip almost 400 kilometers from Yaoundé.

When I was sure they were gone, I went upstairs to ask my neighbor, Kiki, a woman from Madagascar, if she would sit with my still-sleeping children – while I ran a few errands.

Catching my breath, I took a taxi to the American Embassy to confirm that the two U.S. AID employees, Jim and Bob, were planning to meet me in Maroua – Cameroon Airline's northern stop. Everything was all set. I collected my tickets, which I had stored for safe-keeping at the Embassy. On the way back to Tschinga, I attempted to locate Mikita, our housekeeper, to let her know she didn't have to work that day. I never found her.

Arriving back in Tschinga, I looked up at the curtains hanging from the patio doors. They were made with a bright fabric purchased at one of the local markets, and picked out by Christopher. The curtains were tailored by someone unknown to me -- a mystery woman. Chris thought they were stunning. The orange and mustard yellow and brown rounded figures looked like small hamburgers sitting sideways, stacked in long vertical rows. They were loud and obnoxious – pretty gaudy.

It was around 7:00 or so on that rainy May morning when I told myself to end all my looking around and remembering and to start thinking about my plan – what was coming next. I very cautiously allowed myself about an hour before packing – just in case John and Christopher returned for some forgotten item.

While my children slept, I sorted through their clothing, stuffing in just the most essential items. Trembling, I collected many of our photos. I woke up Fitemi and Bentasi, instructing them to hurry and bathe and dress, for we were going on a trip to North Cameroon. They were excited.

Fitemi wore her red and yellow tie-dyed midi-skirt with a white peasant blouse. I laid out Bentasi's brown corduroy slacks and blue knit shirt. I bathed Sarikki and dressed him in a taupe corduroy overall and aqua-green silk button-down shirt.

One of Rikki's little red leather shoes was missing! Frenzied, I searched and searched but couldn't find it. Thinking it might be at Esther's place, forgotten after the party the day before, I picked up our satchel and hailed a taxi. We headed to Cité Verte, hoping to collect Rikki's shoe.

When I arrived at Esther's place, she was in a "tizzy" – getting ready to come see me in Tschinga! But why? Esther just found out her husband's brother, Nicholas, was flying to Garoua – and that he would be on the plane with me! Nicholas was a Cameroonian border officer. Esther was worried, thinking my escape might be discovered. At that point, I was very calm. I knew what I had to do. Nothing was going to shake me. I told Esther to compose herself, for if she didn't become more level-headed, she would give her relatives a reason to be suspicious. I never found Rikki's shoe; I told myself he was young enough to travel barefoot without arousing too much suspicion.

As I had carefully planned out weeks before, I took a taxi to the home of my friends, Ron and Helen, employees at the British Embassy. They had graciously offered to drive us to the Yaoundé Airport. Ron had warned me not to involve anyone from the American Embassy, since an illegal exit would reflect negatively on any Americans involved.

Ron dropped us off at the airport. We boarded a Cameroonian Airlines plane bound for Maroua. On the plane, I immediately spotted Esther's brother-in-law. I strolled over and greeted Nicholas, craftily making up a believable story – that I was headed for a work assignment up in northern Cameroon, sponsored by U.S. AID. Out of a sense of survival, I had become a pretty skilled liar when it was needed.

The flight was short. I was nervous but hid it well. The plane stopped in Garoua, and Nick got off, which was fortunate. We stayed aboard and flew on to Maroua Salak Airport. We landed in less than an hour, near the Mandara Mountains' foothills. Maroua, the largest city in the northern part of Cameroon, is located along the Kaliao River. The hot and dry Sahelian climate was the opposite of that in Yaoundé. There was a lot of activity on the outskirts of the city since Maroua was an important marketing center. The inhabitants were much taller than the Cameroonians I was accustomed to seeing in Tschinga. Those northern folks looked a lot like my children – for the major ethnicity was Fulbe and/or Fulani. I found a taxi, and I headed to the city center to locate the U.S. AID post.

Because of some slip-up or lack of communication, the U.S. AID guys I was scheduled to meet in Maroua were not there! I started to get scared. My imagination played tricks on me – I thought I saw my husband walking out of the Fotambo off-license bar near the center of Maroua!

Stress was having its way with me. What could have gone wrong? Jim and Bob were supposed to drive me to the border. I had no way to find out what had happened. There was no reliable means of communication in Cameroon and almost no links at all in the north. I didn't know what to do. There was no vehicle for my transportation. I didn't even know where the damn border was! I was devastated.

How would I get to Chad without transport? And Sarikki was so fussy. He was shrieking. Trying to locate something for him to eat, I found some *la viande de boeuf* (dried beef) and cornmeal porridge at a roadside stand outside the hotel. Fitemi and Bentasi were arguing and picking at each other, frustrated by my state of mind and from the long journey.

I checked into the *La Kempi Hotel*, put the kids to bed, and sobbed all night. The *Kempi* was not in my plan; luckily, Dad had sent me more money than I asked for. I had come too far to give up now.

The night strung out endlessly. I couldn't fall asleep. Every sound shattered my nerves. The symphony of the desert added a new dimension – there were subtle chirps and rustling sounds – producing an unsettling evening chorus. The hours flipped to a nocturnal world. Picking up and reading a *la Kempi Hotel* pamphlet describing the flora and fauna of north Cameroon, I imagined all sorts of things -- a kangaroo rat hustling to avoid snakes and owls, a mule deer sitting close to my window, owls on the lowest alcove overlooking the Raphia palms, and "song dogs" yipping and barking wild ditties. Sleep never came.

If I was unsuccessful crossing over the Chari, and was discovered and escorted back to Yaoundé with my children, Chris would be eternally irate, squeezing every ounce of life out of me. One chance was all I was going to get! Knowing about how transit operated in Cameroon, I convinced myself to try absconding alone. I figured that I could manage to get to Kousseri, close to the Chari River separating Cameroon and Chad, but after that, I would have to improvise.

Before dawn, we left for Maroua's local transport park. There was no alternative but to travel by bush taxi – the only way to get around in central and western Africa. It's the most basic and raw transport in existence – a private van run by local transport park drivers. Those vans had a capacity of eight to twelve, max. But I never rode in one with less than thirteen or fourteen. One of the nicknames for a bush taxi was a *brousse,* another was *sept places* – "seven places" – which was misleading since there were always more than seven riders. We waited and waited for the taxi driver to let us board his rusty old van. In his mind, there had to be plenty of folks waiting in line to over-stuff his bus. That sour-faced chauffeur did not budge until he determined enough passengers needed his transport services. After two hours, enough riders appeared to fill that *brousse.*

Fitemi, Bentasi, Sarikki, and I climbed into an over-crowded dirty gray VW bus christened with the inscription *"Desert Rat"* in large sooty letters. The van came complete with natural air conditioning – the only glass was the cracked sheet above the dashboard. The *brousse* ride through arid North Cameroon was horrendous. The moniker *brousse* is translated as "bushfire" in English – very appropriate. Hot desert air whipped around our heads, coating our tense, restless bodies with dirt and sand. I listened to rustling winds and screeching flying fowl. When the driver stopped to rest, lizards and insects scurried and flew around the grimy *Desert Rat* in every direction. But mostly, the desert was the sound of silence – eerie.

We bounced over rugged terrain and bad roads with no water to drink. Piquant ginger beer was the only beverage available -- so I allowed my children their first try at beer! Packed in like cattle. Foul smells. Goats. Heat. Chickens. Lice. Diarrhea. Thirst. The passengers were amazingly cheerful in spite of all the discomfort. All the travelers were kind and helpful to me and my kids. A striking young Fulani woman held Sarikki for me. An older gentleman played Sobol with Bentasi and

Fitemi. It was impossible for the wooden board and seeds to stay still long enough for them to play easily, but they had fun trying. We were covered with flies. It was difficult to stay hydrated.

I wondered if my unborn child could survive the jolts and the heat – and especially the parching lack of water! My discomfort was exacerbated by the unsureness of my ability to get across the Chari River into neighboring Chad. We arrived in a deserted area with few vehicles in sight. Sweat rolled down our faces. Sarikki slept in my arms, glued against me with sand and perspiration.

Kousseri, known as Mser, was in sight. It was a city in the Far North Province, the capital of the Logone-et-Chari department. Upon arrival, we saw many markets with women selling plantains, ground nuts, coco yams, and cassava; some were even set up to serve the famous *Mbongo Tchobi*, a spicy black bean stew.

I asked a stranger in a nearby off-license bar for directions to the border depot. Following the directions I was given, Fitemi, Bentasi, and I walked for many kilometers through rocks, stones, ruts, and scalding sand. I was loaded down with my bulky satchel on my right arm and Sarikki, a heavy toddler, on my left. I was frightened and fatigued and weak. We all felt nauseous. By the time I could discern the river's nearness, the kids were restless and grumbling.

"There's a taxi," Fitemi shouted, panting!

We all yelled for the driver to stop. As we tried to open the taxi door, the driver held up his hand, signaling for us to wait. I had forgotten that Cameroonian taxis often lacked door handles – to allow the driver to have total control over who entered his cab. He reached back and opened the back passenger door for us to get in. Whew! We all scurried inside and enjoyed a short rest. When the border station was in sight, I felt the heavy humidity of the Chari hanging in the air.

"*Bonjour mes amies,*" I spoke as clearly as I could, greeting the border officials.

They smiled and waved me on. Miraculously, we passed through the first station of the border headquarters quite effortlessly. I paid the taxi driver, and we exited the cab and continued on foot. We walked into the next station, and I nervously presented my "second" passport. Luckily, I had declared my passport lost when I was in Yaoundé – so I didn't have to give the guards my original passport. A young border official commanded us to sit down and wait, pointing to the entrance.

I looked around and saw a huge Cameroonian flag hanging above the border doorway – with its striking tri-colors of green, red, and yellow and the yellow five-pointed star in its center. It was battered and torn – barely moving in the heat. I hoped we could pass through that post; I prayed we could get around the Cameroonian laws!

The customs officer motioned for us to enter. We sat down on three rickety old three-legged stools under some wooden tribal-mask sculptures -- which looked like Fulani warriors. I noticed ten or more empty bottles of *33 Export* and *Castel* beer beneath the art forms.

One of the officers called me, and I was questioned extensively – in French, of course. My French language skills weren't that good, so I acted as if I could speak only English. I tried not to show my shakiness. Being pregnant, I pointed to my large stomach, and I asked the border guards to let me use the outhouse. Thank God they were quite drunk – and therefore utterly agreeable!

When the guards were boisterously conversing together and out of sight, I picked up Sarikki and clutched him firmly against my chest. Pushing Bentasi and Fitemi ahead of me, we scampered down the hill towards the latrine, scurrying toward the river – at least a hundred meters away! I could not feel my feet.

Then I saw the banks of the Chari! I could feel its freshness. Nervous and exhausted, I handed a young Cameroonian fisherman 20,000 francs CFA and pleaded with him to row us across the river to N'Djamena, the capitol city of Chad. He tossed my bag into his dugout canoe, and we climbed in.

The bottom of the canoe was partly dirt but mostly rotted wooden planks. Rusty steel braces held the canoe loosely together. We plopped down onto the floor straddled between our satchel and a pile of smelly tiger fish. Spotting a crocodile sunning itself on the shore, Bentasi pointed and yelled, "Mom, look!"

Fitemi and Bentasi playfully dragged their sand-coated hands and arms in the river's waters. Sarikki was sleeping, looking peaceful and content; I sprinkled tiny droplets of water on his chubby little face to cool him down. He woke up, smiling. The water brought relief both physically and mentally. We were on our way to Chad, moving across the beautiful Chari River in a dugout canoe!

I made it – with all my children. I survived.

> *he frightened me – drew blood and tears;*
> *he was a callous man;*
> *the chains he tightened, cold and firm;*
> *he bound my feet and hands*
> *I can't remember every act he did to keep control*
> *so, in my mind, I built a plan –*
> *deliverance my goal*
>
> *(from "A New Beginning" by Joy Klaaren Forgwe)*

Chad was probably the worst place to cross over the border, for soldiers patrolled the abandoned roadways, and bullet markings randomly decorated N'Djamena's buildings. The civil war was ongoing. My plan was not the best one – but it worked.

What I knew about the conflict I had just walked into was that it had been waged by rebel factions against two different Chadian governments. The first was led by Chad's first president, Françoise Tombalbaye, quite an authoritarian leader. I did remember that Tombalbaye was murdered by his own army. A military government emerged, led by Malloum – who had just, in the last month or so, stepped down. I did not know what was presently happening in N'Djamena. I thought that either the United Nations or an organization of the United African States was hoping to establish a balance between the Southerners and the rest of the country.

The American Ambassador had been evacuated to the U.S. A couple of *gendarmes* gave me the directions I needed, and after a long walk, we arrived at the American Embassy – only to find it practically abandoned. The Vice Consul back in Cameroon had given me the name of her counterpart in N'Djamena, assuring me that she would provide housing for us and transportation to purchase food, my tickets to the U.S., and anything else I needed. But, of course, she wasn't there – the Chadian Vice Consul had been evacuated, temporarily, to Cameroon. Now what?

Fitemi and Bentasi were exhausted, plus they were not feeling well at all – most likely because their stomachs were empty. Sarikki had diarrhea. We were tired and dirty and sore from walking ungodly long distances with our heavy belongings. We needed to find a place to sit and rest. Thankfully, there were a few folks working around the embassy compound. A couple Frenchmen assisted us, and with instructions from someone who was still running the embassy in spite of everything going on, we were sent off somewhere to sleep.

Wow! I don't know how it happened, but we were lodged in the U.S. AID director's abandoned villa, a huge compound which included a drained swimming pool – to remind me, perhaps, that the residents had been made to leave. A Chadian guard was posted by the front door. The main floor of the spacious villa was barren except for a few sheet-encased chairs and sofas. On the second floor were multiple bedrooms and a number of abandoned beds, lacking any sheets or other bed covers but artistically bordered with carved headboards. We gleefully anticipated sleeping on those bare mattresses, for it was all about perspective – snug and cozy compared to meager traveling accommodations, or lack thereof. The kitchen was huge, with no food to cook.

The guard transported us to the American Embassy's commissary the next day, and I purchased some rations – all unlabeled canned goods, the only food available. Returning to the compound's kitchen, Fitemi and Bentasi had fun opening the unmarked cans, not knowing their contents. They made a game of it. Most of the canned goods were baked beans or various soups; Bentasi cheered every time he found tuna fish! Daily I hoped we would be able to fly out of Chad and on to Europe – but the civil conflict in Chad delayed our travels.

To occupy time while my kids played, I climbed up the stairs to the third floor, where I discovered a shelf containing forgotten mysteries. My next days were spent reading The Maltese Falcon. When I had read enough mystery and intrigue, I went outside to walk around the beautiful yard. To my surprise, the plants and bushes were neatly labeled. Particularly striking were the bright red flowers of the *Royal Poinciana*, known as the "flamboyant tree." I dreamed that one day I would have a garden like that.

As I tried to concentrate, my thoughts were on the condition of my unborn child. My travels had been stressful and filled with poor nutrition and lack of sleep. The bush taxi ride shook my body around a lot. Could my baby endure that? My thoughts continued to be on my baby coming in a few months, for I had not received any medical care since becoming pregnant. And the climate in N'Djamena was so hot and dry that when I washed Sarikki's diapers they dried as I hung them up.

We stayed in N'Djamena for about three weeks. I feared Christopher would discover my point of departure at the Chari riverbank and locate us in Chad. Countless times, we traveled to the airport hoping to fly out, only to be disappointed. Because of the warfare in Chad, very few regularly scheduled planes were flying in or out. We watched military vehicles arrive and depart. And to complicate matters, DC-10s were the normal airplanes used in Chad – and for some safety reasons, they were temporarily grounded in the summer of 1979. After three weeks, we boarded a DC-8. The American Embassy displaced four passengers to give us some seats. We were headed to Paris and then home! When I told Fitemi and Bentasi we were returning to Michigan, they exploded with excitement.

Sitting on that DC-8, I wondered what Christopher was doing. Had he returned from his home in Bamenda? Was he searching for us? As I reflected on the differences between Cameroon and the U.S., I saw that Chris embraced the very dubious facets of both worlds. I was relieved to be away from his command – and on my way to a new life.

Our late arrival in France necessitated staying overnight in Paris. The airline provided a hotel, and we enjoyed ourselves. Early the next morning, we were driven to the terminal; while in DeGaulle Airport, my kids jumped up and down, talking non-stop about seeing their grandparents. On board the plane, Fitemi became acquainted with a young girl across the aisle who looked to be about her age. They enjoyed themselves, laughing and giggling. Bentasi, a rambunctious five-year-old, was teasing his younger brother Sarikki, a rowdy toddler. They were all quite noisy, definitely having a good time. A movie was playing on our TWA flight, and some passengers were irritated with the noise my children were making. I remembered the bush taxi ride through the northern desert area when many very kind and compassionate Cameroonian folks helped me comfort and entertain my energetic children. Now, it was different. I was expected to keep my kids quiet so the other passengers could hear the movie. Many things about Cameroon I missed. I missed the people. I missed the fun. I missed the ravishing countryside. I missed my family and friends.

But I did not miss Christopher.

CHAPTER 6

Parenting Alone: Bewilderment to a New Beginning

G ene and Jonathan picked us up in New York City at Kennedy Airport. I was shaking with many emotions as my brother and I embraced and cried and laughed! The kids were jumping up and down with excitement. We were all amazed how grown-up Jonathan was – now a handsome teenager.

My brother joyously yelled out, "It's a miracle!"

To me, too, it was miraculous; but it was not all jubilation – I was saddened by leaving my Cameroonian friends and family so suddenly – though I had no other path nor choice. My departure from Christopher was overdue.

Stepping out of JFK's terminal into New York City's massiveness, culture shock revisited me. The noise and lights and din of vehicles, expressways, and skyscrapers were overwhelming – with the city's gigantic and intricate web of freeways and parkways and highways. I had become accustomed to the quiet and peaceful countryside of central and western Africa. Now, I had to refocus – assimilating back to my own country and culture.

We spent a lovely week with my brother and his family. Kristen and Joshua, 12 and 9 now, had grown and matured. They smiled when they laid eyes on their newest little cousin; Sarikki quickly became the hub of everyone's attention – and he adored it. Fitemi and Bentasi were treated royally by their Connecticut cousins. I slept and relaxed, wrapped up in my sweet sister-in-law's cozy afghan. Mary and Gene made certain we were comfortable.

We stayed up late many nights, talking and laughing and telling stories. On our second day in Middletown, my brother's passport arrived by post. Dad had instructed Gene to ready himself to fly to Cameroon – just in case I needed help. I was touched. The following week, Gene drove us to Springfield, Massachusetts, and my children and I boarded a train bound for west Michigan. I longed to see my parents and friends. But I was a bit anxious. Raising four children alone. As I rode that overnight train, I had time to reflect while my children slept. I thought about how I had continued my cataclysmic relationship with Christopher, how I had continued to allow myself to be abused and devalued. It took me too long to say "no more!" If only I could have, as I had dreamed, made some sun shine on my marriage. So many unpleasant memories erased the pleasant ones.

The train stopped somewhere in mid-Pennsylvania, and the kids woke up. My mind bounced back into the present. I was eagerly anticipating renewing my bonds with family and friends. My brother, Keith, picked us up in Toledo. It was great to see him – he had not changed at all since the brisk autumn day that I left for Cameroon. He was the same friendly, supportive brother. – and, of course, he was still a legendary Italian car enthusiast. Keith transported us to Holland. I debated whether to settle in East Lansing or Holland. East Lansing, being a university town, would be more enjoyable and a better fit for my diverse family, but Holland and the west Michigan area would be more practical, for my parents had retired and bought a house there. It might be helpful to live close to family.

After facing so much life trauma, my first moments with Mom and Dad were tear-jerking. They were relieved that all of us had arrived safely. Dad, Mom, Keith, and I talked and laughed and cried for hours – making the most of our family reunion. Fitemi and Bentasi crawled all over Uncle Keith and Grandma and Grandpa, barely giving them room to breathe – and they all gloried in it. Sarikki entertained the entire clan, definitely enjoying the attention.

When everyone settled down, I spent some time telephoning old friends. My comrade, Pat Simpson, came right over to see us and get her first peek at Sarikki. Pat hurried up the stairs to look at Rikki's little cherub-like face while he slept in Mom's Jenny Linn bed. Pat picked him up affectionately, and we all drove over to see Pat's sister, Bobbie. It was great rekindling old friendships.

My second day back in Michigan, Christopher called. He talked with Mom. I chose to not speak with him. It wasn't long before I received a letter from my dear sister-in-law, MaryAnn. She was so upset. I knew she would be. I wished I could have talked with her before I left Yaoundé -- but I could not put her in that position between her brother and me. MaryAnn was boiling over with exasperation. I felt so sorry for her. I wanted to explain. Would she ever understand? I hauled out Dad's old Royal typewriter, and with tears streaming down my cheeks, I pounded down on those old keys, revealing to MaryAnn many of her eldest brother's abusive and neglectful actions. I was angry with Christopher, I was furious. I was distressed by MaryAnn's letter. I spilled out everything. I posted a similar letter to Mama and Papa Forgwe. I wanted them to understand. It was a heart-rending time.

We stayed with Mom and Dad on 15th Street in Holland for a few weeks. I wanted to have a home of my own, but all my belongings, including my VW bus, which was probably decaying and hidden in the foliage outside Baffousam, were in Cameroon! It would be difficult to set up housekeeping with only a beat-up suitcase, assorted stacks of memorabilia, and a large collection of photos. I resigned myself to temporarily staying with my parents.

With Dad's help and advice, I searched for a competent divorce attorney – one who was well-versed in international law and knowledgeable about "kid-snatching" across international borders. I found a lawyer in Lansing, signed a retainer, and Christopher was served with papers via registered international mail. The divorce decree contained a permanent restraining order. Chris never responded to the papers, but the divorce was granted. I was not able to obtain any alimony or child support – for our court system had no jurisdiction across international boundaries. And even if support was possible, wages in Cameroon were only a fraction of wages in the U.S. Where would the support come from? I was granted, however, the legal ownership of the household articles I had packed and stored in Lansing, Michigan, in 1977. Because the Cameroonian government never paid the storage and shipping charges, which Cameroon was responsible for in accordance with Christopher's U.N. scholarship, our stored goods were never shipped to Cameroon. The fees that accumulated over time were beyond my financial means – for my dollar supply showed a negative balance. My parent's church in Holland offered to pay the overdue bill for me. I was so thankful for their generosity.

Having few resources, I applied for ADC (Aid to Dependent Children). It was granted, and I started getting my life in order. Now that I was eligible for Medicaid, I made an appointment with a gynecologist. My fourth pregnancy had seemed to progress normally – but I had never seen a physician.

Looking for an apartment was a frustrating process. I became aware of the stigma of single parenthood and having lots of kids. I felt like one of those statistics I studied in Sociology 101 – a divorced mom, pregnant, with *x* number of children. I was treated as if it was my life-long desire to live off the generosity of the government. Countless landlords found excuses when they counted the number of children I had. As I trudged from apartment to apartment, I could feel people gaping at me and my bi-racial children. What was running through their minds? When I went on errands, I would sometimes be asked: *"Are they adopted?"* I was able to rise above people's insinuations – maybe because I felt relief, like a breath of fresh air, because life was calmer without Christopher controlling and overpowering me. But to say my life was easy would not be true. I had many roles to play; but at least I was safe and relaxed. I no longer had to pretend. I no longer had to be deceptive. I found a 3-bedroom apartment in Meadowlane Townhouses. It felt good to be settled, especially with a baby coming.

August of 1979 was especially hot and sultry. Since I had already experienced pregnancy coupled with intense heat, I wondered why I was so uncomfortable. I wished school would begin. The kids were restless and needed something new to delve into. Being close to birthing my fourth child and not working, I had a lot of time to think – and many thoughts pestered my mind. I jumped from repulsive thoughts of Christopher to painful memories of my Chicago ordeal to yearnings to see Martin, MaryAnn, Rose and family, Primus, Grace and family, and Papa and Mama Forgwe. I didn't know if I was emotionally ready for another child. I wondered how I would manage. MaryAnn had helped me so much in Cameroon. I longed to see her again.

And then, near the end of August, I received MaryAnn's divine letter. It was so different from her first letter. With her soothing words, MaryAnn handed me some peace.

MaryAnn wrote: *"I can hardly tell you how happy we were to read from you this morning. It has left me crying most of the day, but at least there is one thing that consoles me – that you have some peace now, or you are on your way to having it. God gave you to us, and God took you away. It was all in God's plan."*

I wanted to see her and hug her. MaryAnn understood – I knew she had witnessed many of Christopher's abusive behaviors. She was aware.

Sleeping was difficult that first week of September. I was bigger than a barn, and Rikki, Bentasi, and Fitemi loved to crawl into bed with me. Between the kids and my stomach, I couldn't maneuver. During the daytime, Rikki was into everything. It took a lot of stamina to keep up with him. I expected to deliver my baby in late September. And then, on October 10, I received a telephone call from Juanita, a good friend from Lansing. Juanita was frantic. She said that she saw Christopher walking down Grand River Avenue in East Lansing! I was terrified! I called Jefferson School to make sure Fitemi and Bentasi were allowed to be picked up by only me or my parents. I arranged for my sister, Mary Andersen, to come to Holland to help me while I was in the hospital – whenever that was to be.

My water broke that night, and I promptly telephoned my doctor. Dad drove me to Holland Hospital. I didn't expect anything to go wrong – it was my fourth delivery. Both Bentasi's and Sarikki's entries into the world were quick and relatively easy. While I had experienced a long labor with Fitemi, it was nothing like what I went through with my fourth delivery! My contractions were intense and severe, but I was not dilating – so both my baby and I were in distress. I was tense and nervous because I thought Christopher might appear. And then what!?! An additional physician was rushed into the birthing room. Nurses scurried around, wheeling machines up around my bed. Labor was hard -- unendurable. A fetal monitor was installed. I guess my little girl just didn't want to be born. After more than twenty hours, my beautiful baby girl entered the world!

Christopher never appeared. Juanita must have been mistaken, but I was still surrounded with uncertainty – and a little relief. Two days later, I went home to Meadowlanes with my baby girl. Fitemi, Bentasi, and Sarikki were rolling with enthusiasm to hold cute little Martina Joy. "*Martina*," named after Mama Martina Forgwe. I felt so badly to leave Mama so abruptly – with no explanation. Martina "*Joy*" – named after me. I was parenting by myself now.

My sister drove to Holland from Champaign, Illinois, in order to help me with all the chores and tasks placed on me and my family with a new member; for there were added duties that came with a larger family. I don't think I could have managed without my big sis Mary. I was now responsible for parenting four children – with two of them still in diapers. Both Mary and I were very busy those first weeks I was home with my enlarged little family – we were quite exhausted, yet we thoroughly enjoyed our sister bonding time together.

When Mary left my place and returned to her home in Champaign, the realization that my family had grown to five finally hit me – the Forgwe Five! I cheerfully told myself that I was up to the challenge. My children were my whole world. And, lucky for me, Martina was a content baby. She slept all night right from the very beginning. God must have known that I needed some rest. I felt content as I nursed my new baby girl, encircled by three angelic faces glorying in the arrival of their beautiful baby sister.

Papa Forgwe, not yet knowing of Martina's birth, wrote me in response to my letter posted to him and Mama Forgwe months earlier – my letter in which I tried to explain why I left their eldest son. Papa's words asked me to forgive Christopher again.

Papa wrote, *"Remember what Saint Peter asked our Lord Jesus: How many times must I forgive my brother who has been offending me in so many occasions? Jesus said to him, 'Forgive your brother seven times seven.' So I pray that you, as a Christian will change up your mind and forgive Christopher again. He has promised to change and we are prepared to see that he does so."*

Papa's words made me feel unholy. I started to wonder how I could have taken the kids away from Papa and Mama. Maybe if I had let them help, things could have worked out.

But did I want to spend my life with a man who needed to be controlled and monitored by his parents? Yes, I made the right decision. Days later, another letter arrived – from Christopher.

Christopher's words: *"By now, you have probably come up with the fourth reason for being the most important woman in my life (along with my mother). And even though I have no reason to be hopeful, especially after reading my parents' and MaryAnn's earlier letters, I am hopeful. For one thing, you have named the baby Martina. And what's more your letters to them, in spite of their contents, still emote a sense of love at the bottom of which I expect to find some forgiveness."*

His letter left me baffled! I wondered how Chris would have treated me if I hadn't been able to have children! The "sense of love" Christopher referred to in my letter was the love I felt for his family, not for him. And as for forgiveness, Christopher said he <u>expected</u> it! He was still trying to control me!

Martina was only a few months old when Yolanda called. I was puzzled. She asked if she could come to my apartment to see me. I agreed reluctantly. When she arrived, she was carrying a big brown paper bag. Yolanda placed the bag's contents on my kitchen table, saying something about never wanting to see or hear from Christopher again. She gave me, in a big pile, the letters Christopher wrote to her! I wondered what that drama was all about. Yolanda expounded that her relinquishment of those letters was proof that she was serious about putting off contact with Christopher. She said the letters really belonged to me! I was confused. I had no clue what her motivation was. She did not stay long, only about fifteen minutes – probably because I was very short with her. When she left, I read the letters and postcards, which had been secretly written by Christopher to Yolanda while I was still in Cameroon. Sorting through the pile, I, of course, remembered reading the letters Yolanda wrote to Christopher, the ones delivered to my office at the Ministry of Education. Now, I was seeing yet another perspective.

From the more than a dozen letters and cards, a few of Christopher's words to Yolanda stood out:

"Hello, My Dear Queen of Hearts.

...Oh, how I miss you,

Love From the King of Fire!

Hello Fine Woman,

....I had a welcome that had all the passion and love depicted in the Gospel of the Prodigal Son, along with the splendour of Julius Caesar's triumphant entry into Rome after one of his Gothic Wars.

....I truly miss you. I do all the wishful thinking in the world – enough to have performed all kinds of miracles to bring you to me.

Love, Your Christopher

... The best is yet to come in the summer of our lives.

King of Fire"

As I read Christopher's letters to Yolanda, I realized I was no longer angered or hurt by those words or any of his past associations. I had moved past those feelings. It seemed humorous, yet sad, that Christopher's portrayal of his arrival back in Yaoundé was so different than it really was. I was remembering that dingy hotel room and losing my shoe and nobody meeting us! I still wondered why Yolanda gave me those personal correspondences. She said something about it being a symbolic gesture, but I wasn't sure what she meant by that. I speculated how much worse it could have become for me – if I had not left my husband. I speculated if Chris was sane. He sounded, in those letters, like he wasn't lucid. I would have obviously been an unending roadblock to Christopher's happiness. He would have kept on beating me for not being Yolanda – but he would have never let me go because I produced his four children!

As I re-read the letters, I saw an insecurity in my former husband. Some of the lines and phrases really threw me. *King of Fire!? Queen of Hearts!?* Maybe Yolanda also sensed an insecurity. Was that the reason she gifted them to me? What kind of bolstering of his ego was necessary for him? I thought about his perception of his welcome home – "*all the passion and love depicted in the Gospel of the Prodigal Son along with the splendour of Julius Caesar's triumphant entry into Rome!*" Was Chris for real?

Years passed, and my children grew and blossomed. They became less dependent on me, their mom. Each of them developed beautifully and uniquely, each of them writing bright and new chapters in their lives. They definitely had their own distinctive personalities.

Martina was strong and free-spirited, with a creative flair – even at a very young age. She could have been christened "Ms. Determination!" Sarikki, having many friends all over Holland, was definitely the most easy-going and happy of the four – developing a knack for sports. Bentasi was quite the prolific philosopher – thinking everything through, with lots of discussing and sermonizing. Fitemi was intelligent and wise – with poise and grace. She was "Ms. Independence," handling things perfectly and in her own way. I was truly blessed.

My parents loved to take their grandchildren on outings and little adventures. Oftentimes, they picked them up and went out for "coffee" and goodies. They were regular customers at Copper Kettle and East Russ's Restaurant on 8th Street. Grandma and Grandpa were enthralled with Fitemi, Bentasi, Sarikki, and Martina. Grandma loved to have them spend the night – usually one at a time. Sometimes Grandpa, while driving his Chevy Nova, would prop Sarikki up on his lap! I thought that was very dangerous, but there was no stopping them – Sarikki loved to be with his grandpa. My dad often took long walks with his grandchildren, talking about nature and trees and rivers and picking up walnuts. Every Halloween, Grandma and Grandpa accompanied Fitemi and Bentasi with "trick-or-treating" festivities. Autumn brought hotdogs, roasted marshmallows, and football games. Every Wednesday and Saturday throughout the winter months, Grandpa treated Bentasi and Sarikki to

Hope College basketball games. Fitemi loved to bake chocolate chip cookies and Crispette Squares with Grandma. Bentasi followed Grandpa around his workshop, learning about all his tools and other cool stuff. Martina was fascinated with Grandpa's walnut cracker, and she loved to widely open her mouth when he offered her some nutmeats to chew and devour.

I settled into daily life with all its activities. It was time to move on and improve my living situation. The Forgwe family had grown beyond our tiny Meadowlands apartment, so I rented a grisly yellow house on West 16th Street, across the street from E.E. Fell Middle School. With the support of a small scholarship, I began studying for a master's degree in Public Administration at Grand Valley State, hoping to prepare for work in an international setting. I studied hard and attended classes religiously. I felt pretty good about myself. School was a great outlet; I met with fellow classmates for weekly study sessions in my living room. My study-mates and I commuted to the Allendale campus twice weekly, and we enjoyed our graduate classes and our friendships. School kept me focused. I did most of my studying and homework during the daytime while Fitemi and Bentasi were in school.

It wasn't long before I became acquainted with my next-door neighbor, Laurie. We became friends quite quickly. She helped me with little chores around my place – and with kid care. When Rikki and Tasi painted blue dinosaurs on their bedroom wall, it was Laurie who helped me clean up the mess. It was great to have her friendship and support.

And in addition, Mom had a church friend whose recently divorced daughter had just bought a house in Holland. Mom introduced me to Linda and her six children. The seven of them lived only a block away from me. Linda was also a single parent. We often spent time together while our ten children played and got acquainted. Linda's life, like mine, had been a struggle – but she had a very positive attitude. We became comrades, sharing not only our setbacks but also our hopes and dreams. Linda encouraged me to attend a divorce-coping seminar or at least talk to a counselor. I decided I didn't need a counselor or a seminar.

My new-found friends gave me lots of support, for which I was appreciative, and advice – which I didn't always heed. I felt that my life with Christopher had been so difficult that now I was doing great. Since I had been through hell, I thought I could endure whatever life threw at me.

And I felt that my biggest problem was my extra weight. OMG! That never-ending war of weight! I had tried many strategies to find something that worked for me. I knew that rewarding myself with food was not the ticket to happiness. I had to learn to change my life style, but how? Oftentimes, I managed to take off many pounds – only to add them back, plus some additional ones, later. That battle went on most of my life. I figured if I could rid myself of all that unattractive fat, I could do anything.

I did do "okay" for quite a long time. I handled life's little ups and downs well. Maneuvering daily tasks was difficult, but I made it manageable – waking up early, kids off to school, laundry, cooking, vacuuming, car-pooling, piano lessons, studying, violin lessons, soccer games, French lessons, car maintenance, football games, dishes, picking up the little messes, basketball, and on and on. There was no time to rest. Life with four was constantly bustling – even when everything was progressing normally.

But there were more self-defeating behaviors I was operating under. What about my smoking? I tried to not light up around my children, but of course, they knew. How were they going to handle a mother who could not control her eating and the terrible, life-sucking smoking?

Midst these behaviors, I was trying to be an understanding parent with struggles my children faced. When Fitemi was only in the third grade, she came home crying after school one day. When I tried to comfort her, she told me a cranky old man on Harrison Street yelled out at her, "we don't want no niggers on our grass," as she passed by his house! OMG!

That was one of numerous and ongoing racial incidents we have had to deal with. No one ever learns how to handle these outrageous words and actions. They grind away at you, squeezing the very core of your being.

My children have, many times, been put on the fringes of society. It's hard for many people to understand this, for perhaps it has never been a part of their own experience. It was never, before, part of mine. As a child, I was always accepted in school, at church, and on the playground. I'm not saying that I didn't have problems, such as skirmishes with friends, misunderstandings with teachers, etc. – for I did. Everyone does. In many situations I did not act wisely – I didn't always make the best choices – so I suffered some embarrassments or reprimands because of my CHOICES. But I never suffered anything because of WHO I WAS! That is the big difference. I have seen my children suffer because of the color of their skin.

I did not handle that stuff life threw at us very well. I'm speaking of encounters with the prejudice and meanness aimed at my kids! I'm talking about having to deal with Fitemi being put in the back of her class. And the list goes on.

And in addition, I was trying to handle life without intimacy and coping with never-ending financial difficulties. With these "bigger" problems, I needed some help. My "help" was nothing but a hindrance. I worked and ate and laughed and ate and toiled and ate and cosmetically enjoyed life, but I needed more. Food was my comfort. I didn't realize how much anger and pain I had inside of me. From time to time, I managed to muster up enough willpower to deprive myself of my favorite foods – and I started to lose a few pounds. I don't remember which program I joined. I think it was Diet Center. But my smoking got worse. I tried not to light up around my children, but there were plenty of other opportunities. Self-defeating behaviors were running and ruining my life.

I felt proud of myself for trimming down. Everyone encouraged me. "Joy, you look so good. Just watch out. Men will start hanging around." A gentleman from East Lansing indicated an interest in dating me. School became more difficult. The kids got more difficult. It seemed like I just sort of gave up – or gave in. Before I could catch myself, I gained back most of the weight I had lost! Life was a paradox – I felt terrible, yet I was safe.

I see-sawed back and forth between size 14 and size 4x at least three, maybe four, times. I stopped smoking, and then I found a reason to begin again – smoking, that is. I asked myself why. But I would always find an excuse. I was much too busy to worry about myself. I involved myself in my kids' lives, my friends' lives, and my schoolwork. I was lonely – but I didn't really want the hassle that a relationship entailed. I was busy enough. I felt I was fine. I could survive by myself. I had lived through enough bad times to be able to function pretty well alone.

Before I could finish my master's degree, Social Services pressured me into finding a job. I went about the business of job hunting – in addition to child rearing and performing all the duties associated with being the head of a household. My schooling had to go on hold. Government programs do not work well for every situation. If I could have continued my education, I could have been better prepared for the work world.

With four creative and curious children, life was more than full! I continued to juggle school schedules with lessons, sports, and on and on. I became acquainted with their teachers at both Van Raalte and Jefferson Elementary schools. My youngsters spent many years growing and maturing in those charming institutions. They were all good students – and they loved their school activities. I didn't do much for myself, however. I extracted my self-esteem from my children's accomplishments. They were vibrant children, and their successes made me feel like I was flourishing.

In the early 1980's, my parents enabled me to buy a small cape cod house on the west side of Holland; Mom and Dad purchased the home and sold it to me on a very reasonable land contract. They were very generous. Dad and I had fun fixing, painting, and decorating – generally making ends meet with our creativity. Those were very busy times, but they were good years – full of inventiveness, school, work, and family.

In August I accepted a position as the Office Manager of the Department of Economics and Business Administration at Hope College. In those early years on my new job, I worked a lot of overtime – nights and week-ends. There was never enough money, and I couldn't afford to pass up work opportunities.

My next-door neighbors -- just across the driveway -- were very helpful and loving. Many times Brenda cared for and fed my kids when I was feeling "blue," occupied with the care of my elderly parents, or working extra hours to "make ends meet." Brenda was an angel. I thank God for her and her family.

I longed for more quality time with my children; I was experiencing the many time constraints of being a single parent and a working mom. I had no time to think about doing anything for myself. But I continued to function well in spite of the fatigue. I still had a passion for life – and I generally was pretty adept at facing my multiple responsibilities with a full-time job and a full-time agenda at home. I can see now that all that "busyness" made it impossible for my emotions to surface.

My position at Hope College was a "God-send" for me. Working hard and being appreciated gave me the strokes I needed to go on. I loved my job, especially because I was good at it. I landed the job at a time when computers were just beginning to be used. No one knew how to operate the digital DEC-mate word processor that had just been delivered to the Econ/Bus Dept. in the Sligh Building. I took the learning tapes home – and I organized an office that was looking for order. I was in the right place at the right time. And I had all the right skills. I was extremely busy, for my department was one of the largest on Hope's campus. I loved the people I worked with, and I prized being productive. My job evaluations were always good, like this comment from one faculty member, *"Letters of evaluation in Joy's file testify to our utter amazement that one person could ever do all this, let alone with such excellence, grace, and good humor. What a pleasure Joy is to work with."*

I received lots of support and TLC from the many student workers I supervised. Many of those young coeds enjoyed dropping over at my place to visit, play euchre, and interact with my kids. Jackie, whom I met in 1982, actually became a part of our family unit -- preparing scrumptious meals for us to enjoy, going on exciting outings to the Michigan beaches, and warmly interacting with Fitemi, Bentasi, Sarikki, and Martina.

Even though I appeared to be operating quite smoothly, I was troubled – routinely afflicted by nightmares about my freshman year at Hope College. How did I end up working at the very place I had been trying to forget? I couldn't let go of that terror. Sometimes, I managed to push my bad dreams into the background by becoming obsessed with my still lingering anger towards Christopher. He wrote me some accusatory letters – demeaning me for abandoning him. He could never see his part in any of that.

Even though I wanted to forget about Chris, I had studied a lot of psychology, and I believed my kids should know about their heritage and their father. I thought it would be wise for Martina, Sarikki, Bentasi, and Fitemi to have a familial connection with their Cameroonian grandparents, aunts, uncles, nephews, nieces, and many cousins. I believed it would be unwise for them to grow up without knowing where they came from. I wanted them to be able to stay in contact with their entire family. It was going to take work – and it meant some dreaded contact between Christopher and me. I let Christopher know that I believed he and his family should correspond with Fitemi, Bentasi, Sarikki, and Martina.

In April of 1983, Chris telephoned. I spoke with him – relaying family information about schools and activities. A letter from Christopher followed the phone call. The lengthy letter told me a lot about what Christopher was doing; he seemed to be bragging. Chris tended to go on and on about himself. There were times that he saw himself as some sort of a god. I should not have been so cordial to him on the phone the night he called, for he interpreted my agreeable mood to be some kind of indication of hope for a reunion. I responded to his letter and let him know I had no desire to renew our relationship. We were divorced and incompatible. My goal was to keep communication lines open among him and our children. I waited and waited for him to contact his children.

My friends encouraged me to throw myself into the dating scene, but I held back. I pretty much kept to myself, denying any yearning for companionship and intimacy. Instead, I endeavored to make certain my children were happy and cared for properly. I enjoyed them enormously. I tried to teach them to be loving and to love themselves. I don't believe I was very successful in those endeavors because I had a hard time caring about myself. But in spite of beating myself up, I carried on with a pretty cheerful attitude. There were many times, however, that I craved intimacy – the kind of tenderness that comes from a total sharing with another person. The weight war went on as if that was my biggest liability. I lost many pounds many times. I don't remember the exact details because I worked hard at forgetting the intervals when I gained the weight back. It seemed like every time I would reap the benefits of my amazing willpower, I would cave in and retreat to my original size. I continued that pattern for quite some time – in fact, it became a routine with me. And my smoking wasn't getting any better either. I did, however, try to keep it away from my kids – but I was not successful. I have carried those habits with me.

Soon, I was living with adolescents who were trying to separate from me and grow up. I knew that was a normal process, but knowing and experiencing are two different things.

Fitemi was blossoming, but I was almost too busy to notice. Almost effortlessly, she whizzed through her schooling with mostly A's. In the 5th grade, she studied the violin; then she started playing flute in 6th grade. Her music teacher said she had "perfect pitch!" When Fitemi began high school, I bought her an open-hole flute; it was expensive, but she was so musically talented I believed it would challenge her. Fitemi was very attractive, but it seemed that she didn't think so. There were times she acted out a bit, and I wondered if that acting out could be because when she was only seven, Fitemi witnessed many of her father's abusive actions. Fitemi excelled in school, and when she was a junior in high school, she applied and was selected by the Holland Rotary Club to be an exchange student for her senior year. She traveled to Paris at age sixteen, the beginning of her last year in high school. Fitemi discovered her gift for learning languages. It changed her life. I'm proud of her.

Bentasi – my eldest son who always loved to talk, and had many friends from various diverse backgrounds. He always helped me with household chores, and he liked doing odd jobs around home. Tasi was very easy-going. But when one of his teachers signed him up for a general math class instead of algebra, Bentasi was upset. I remember that he begged me to ask the principal to let him take algebra so he could prepare for college. Bentasi entered an Algebra I class the second semester, lacking the knowledge from the first semester. He finished the class but with difficulty. The following term he worked and studied very hard – and Tasi earned a grade of "A" in Algebra II. Bentasi was very methodical and serious about school. Toward the end of high school, Tasi grew into a very large fellow – more than six feet tall and weighing around 200 pounds. Neither Bentasi nor I were prepared for many people's ignorance. As a young black male living in a predominantly white community, he was oftentimes considered a threat. He routinely experienced paranoid citizens – including police officers. That perception considerably affected his life. Bentasi managed to handle most situations with great pizzazz however – and I'm proud of him.

Sarikki – always happy and content. Always in a good mood. Always a smile, willing to do more than his share. Sports were what interested Rikki – not schoolwork. His "being," at some point, became synonymous with athletics. Sarikki lived for "hoops" and soccer and football – and he possessed natural talent and flair for all athletics. But Sarikki, too, was a black male, and he came across many of the same difficulties encountered by his older brother. I remember the time a police officer stopped Rikki on 15th Street and tossed him into his police car! Sarikki was assisting Uncle Keith by pushing his uncle's motorcycle to East 15th St. – Rikki's grandma and grandpa's house. When the policeman saw Sarikki, the officer saw what he wanted to see – a young black boy who, in the cop's mind, probably stole a bike! Sarikki, too, has been affected by small-mindedness and racism. Sarikki always handled himself with cheerfulness and a great attitude. Rikki was always happy to be himself, and I'm proud of him.

Martina, my sensitive, talented youngest daughter – a pillar of creativity. Martina enjoyed writing and acting. She wrote quite a few stories that demonstrated her intelligence and innovation. I remember her book, <u>The Mitten</u>, which she wrote and illustrated in 3rd grade; it won a book prize. The play Martina wrote in 4th grade was quite the hit! When Martina was eight years old, she thought she was perfect. She wrote: "*I am so perfect. I do everything right. I get all my work right in school. I think school is fun because I am so perfect that it is fun. At home I don't get yelled at, except from my sister, Fitemi. I can't help it I'm perfect.*" If only Martina could have "held on" to that conception of herself throughout her teenage years. For a while, she forgot how smart she was. She was often unhappy and discontented, begging me to buy her the newest styles and fashions. But she never repressed her feelings and perceptions – she was fiercely frank. Martina worked very hard and said exactly what was on her mind, and I'm proud of her.

I did not want Fitemi, Bentasi, Sarikki, and Martina to grow up without their father. I intended for them to spend many of their developing years in Cameroon, somewhat tucked away from the disease of racism. I wanted them to have the advantageous perspective of witnessing a healthy, loving relationship between two people who cared for themselves and for each other deeply. Something had gone amiss. That loving relationship never existed. I could not wish it into being.

Life is rarely neat and easy and smooth. Accepting the choices my children make can sometimes be challenging. I have dreams for them – and I know I must separate my dreams for them from their dreams for themselves.

I made mistakes, and I would like to save Fitemi, Bentasi, Sarikki, and Martina from the kind of trouble I created for myself by my lack of wisdom and judgment. I want my kids to be whole, healthy, happy beings all of their lives. But oftentimes, my ideas about what it takes to be whole and healthy and happy conflict with theirs.

It has taken me years to realize that I cannot make things snug and comfortable for my children or anyone else. Everyone needs to find their own way. I often show and tell my children that I love them very much – and that I know they are intelligent, creative, beautiful and, loving, and strong enough to make things work out for themselves. They know I will always be there for them, but they need to carve out and shape their own lives. It has taken me a good amount of time to realize that I am not responsible for anyone else's bewilderment. I am responsible for myself, however.

We all tried to roll with life's ups and downs. We went on from year to year. My children received little contact from their father. After a while, the kids stopped asking about him. We had contact with the Forgwe family, however. One summer evening, I received a call from Nick, the husband of Grace, Christopher's oldest sister. Nick was in Chicago visiting the family members who had hosted him during his education. He came by bus to visit us. When the children went to sleep, Nick and I talked and laughed and conversed into the early morning hours. Nick was amazed to learn that Christopher and I were divorced. Apparently, Chris had never revealed that information to any of his family. What!?! Nick told me that Christopher had informed family and friends back in Cameroon that I was studying in the U.S. and would eventually be returning to Cameroon. I couldn't believe it. Chris couldn't bring himself to acknowledge what had happened.

On a few occasions after Nick's visit to Holland, the children and I were able to visit with Rose and MaryAnn, Christopher's sisters. They were both living, working, and studying in Massachusetts, in the Boston & Cambridge area.

I fondly recall MaryAnn's visit. I wondered how she would receive me; I worried that she might still be distraught because I did not inform her when I left Cameroon. And I wondered if she was even aware of the divorce! But when she walked through my doorway, it was like we had never been apart. We were both overwhelmed with emotion as we embraced. Tears of happiness flowed down our cheeks, followed by laughs and smiles – and the kids wanted to get in on the action. Hugs and kisses all around! MaryAnn told me now happy she was for me and for her nieces and nephews – happy for our happiness and because we had such a cozy little house and a beautiful family. We had fun visiting, talking, and touring the West Michigan sights – especially the beaches and surrounding sights around Lake Michigan. There were many things to catch up on and not enough time. Fitemi and Bentasi enjoyed their time with her, playing games and proudly showing her their school projects. When introducing her to their friends, they recalled the good times in Cameroon. MaryAnn spent a lot of time getting reacquainted with Sarikki, who was only a toddler when she last held him. Her bond with Rikki was very strong, for she cared for him as a baby while I was working – tying him on her back with a beautifully patterned cotton fabric called an "iro." Sarikki was a big boy, so MaryAnn often reinforced Rikki's back with an additional piece of cloth called an "oja." MaryAnn and little Sarikki were lovingly bound together daily while Auntie laundered clothes, cooked, and did various household errands in and around our Tschinga apartment and yard in Yaoundé. The connection between each of my children and their Auntie was strong.

In the summer of 1993, Rose, just a few years older than MaryAnn, traveled to Cameroon to visit her family. When she returned to the U.S., she brought back letters for all of us from her brother Christopher. He wrote short notes to Fitemi, Bentasi, and Sarikki before, but I didn't recall that Martina ever received her own letter. She glowed when it came. She read it quickly, relaying to me that her daddy's letter was full of longings to see her. Martina, around fourteen at that time, excitedly shared with me that her dad asked her many questions about the music she liked, the television shows she enjoyed, and so on. Less than an hour later, Martina handed me her reply to her father, asking me to mail it:

"September 15, 1993

Dear Dad,

Thank you for the letter. It was very nice of you to write it. I enjoyed reading it and so I decided to write you one too.

I wish I could see you. I can't say that I miss you, since I've never seen you, and I've never had a father figure to compare you with. I always think about the day that I will meet you. I dream about it every night too.

I wish that I could say I love you, but how can you love someone you don't know? How is that possible? I want to visit you so bad but my mother cannot afford it. Oh well, I can dream, can't I"

My mother is so wonderful. I love her so much. I don't know anyone who has a mother as good as mine. She has been there for our family every step of the way and I know she always will be.

On October 11 it will be my birthday. I look a lot older than I am. I look about 16 or 17 and people always mistake me for being that age. I do very good in school and I almost have a 4.0 GPA. Sarikki does pretty good in school, too.

I travel a little, not that much. Sarikki and I did visit Rose and MaryAnn in Boston.

I really don't know what I want to be when I grow up. Maybe a psychologist. I have no idea.

I used to watch the Cosby Show and Different Worlds, but they don't play them anymore because they're kind of old. They have a lot of similar shows like Family Matters and Theo, which is a new show.

I enjoy music by Whitney Houston, Janet Jackson, Mariah Carey, S.W.V. Mary Jo Blige, and I love rap.

My favorite female movie stars are Whoopi Goldberg, Angela Bassett, and Halle Barry. I love Eddie Murphy. He is so funny.

    Anyway, how is Cameroon? How are things going for you? How are your parents?

    Holland has changed a lot since you were here It's expanded. When you were here it was probably almost all white, and now it's not.

    I hope you will write me as soon as you receive this letter. I would really appreciate that. Well, I got to go.

    Love
    Martina"

Martina watched the mail closely for the next few months. I wished I could make Chris write back to her – if only to reply just that one letter. But it never happened. Martina never received a reply.

The others read their letters, but Sarikki seemed to not be too impressed – at least not enough to answer. Bentasi was away at college in Atlanta, Georgia, so I sent his letter to him. Fitemi, however, corresponded with her dad occasionally.

I, too, received a letter. As I read it, I was rather surprised by Christopher's "wanting forgiveness," but I still saw only control surrounding his words:

Christopher wrote, *"I will very much like you to pardon me now and to respond to me even as a forgotten friend. Please forgive me and write me to let me know you have done so."*

Christopher was somewhat repentant, but it was far from good enough. He said in his letter how depressed he was and how much he had suffered, and then he said that we should get back together as a family as God intended and that he expected me to be a dutiful wife and return to him! OMG! Between the lines of Christopher's letter, I sensed what he was thinking. I felt surrounded by control – and I could not breathe. I replied to his letter quickly, writing what flowed out of me – not holding anything back. I wrote as frankly and honestly as I knew how.

I wrote back to Chris, " . . . *I sympathize with what you've been through for the last 14 years. I know you have suffered – and I feel that suffering, too. I don't mean my own suffering. I feel your suffering. I want you to heal – and go on. Broken people aren't of much use to anybody. You can't keep living in a state of depression. Get a hold of yourself. Your talk about us being a family again is far-fetched. You don't even know me. If you thought I was hard to live with 20 years ago, you should see me now. I'm a different person. I've raised four children by myself. You have no idea what that involves. There is no way you will ever understand. And I've changed a lot. I'm a demanding person to live with. I'm overbearing. I don't take orders from anyone. I don't live through anyone. I make my own decisions. I don't tolerate any patrilineal garbage. I go when I want to go. I come when I want to come. I stay when I want to stay. I value relationships – lots of relationships. I desire and work hard on honest relationships. I certainly don't see any "marriage" in the picture for Joy and Christopher. So you might as well kiss that idea goodbye."*

I felt good after I wrote that letter. I was as candid as I could be. I never expected to hear from Chris. I knew that what I said to him was not what he wanted to hear. I never received a reply.

Intertwined with life's daily demands, my kids and I endured more painful encounters with prejudice and bigotry. Somewhere between the time our backyard picnic table was smeared with the malicious words *"we don't want no niggers in our town"* and the time our dining room windows were shattered by a steel pipe, we comprehended the message that we were not a welcomed part of our community.

Those irrational acts of hatred permeated each one of us, building up shields of bitterness. Racism destroys, never builds. Auspiciously, Fitemi, Bentasi and Sarikki seemed to cope with what life dealt them. But were they really coping? They stumbled along the way, but they appeared to be managing. Sometimes, it's difficult to distinguish between moving ahead and escaping. Fitemi followed her dreams to study in France. Bentasi immersed himself in social activities. Sarikki's life was totally involved in sports. It was Martina who found herself sinking into hopelessness. Martina was always full of energy. She was serious about her schoolwork, but seemed to feel "out of place" in the Holland, Michigan area, which had a very homogeneous population. At quite a young age, Martina was quick to challenge implicit biases. She was seeking out, as a teenager, inclusivity for herself and her family.

Did Martina's discontent begin with my tumultuous pregnancy? Maybe while Martina was still in my womb, she could not endure the tensity and stress! I thought of the bumpy bush taxi rides through the desert and the heat and the thirst and the flies. And what about all that anxiety? My heart went out to her -- wanting to help her, understand her, and shield her.

Martina and I had something in common – neither of us were coping very well. We were both despondent, and we quarreled often. Feeling empathetic and hoping to help her, I did many things for Martina. In fact, I threw myself into the middle of her misery. The more I tried to help, the more impetuous Martina became. I don't know when the war between me and Martina began, but it was sometime during her early adolescence. She wanted me to take better care of myself; perhaps she was concerned about losing me. She was definitely disappointed that her father had not answered her letter. In fact, I believe she was devastated. Martina was brutally honest, often pushing friends away from her. She lived a lonely existence for such a young girl.

Before the beginning of middle school, I allowed Martina to move to New Brunswick, New Jersey, and stay with my friend, Linda, where Martina could attend a more diverse school. For the next few years, Martina continued to run from school to school. Her actions pushed me away, but her emotions were intricately connected with mine. Upon returning to Holland, Martina changed schools again. She transferred from Holland to Zeeland Middle School. I drove her, daily, the five miles to Zeeland. It was not easy for Martina to socialize with friends after school, for her new schoolmates were in Zeeland.

I decided to move. I put my house up for sale. But before it sold, I woke up at 5 a.m. to drive Rikki and Martina to Zeeland. I had to sneak out of work at 2:30 p.m. to pick up Martina. Sarikki, heavily involved in sports, wasn't finished until 6:00 or 7:00 p.m. That routine – four daily trips to Zeeland and back – was exhausting, adding strain to my work schedule and home life.

My house didn't sell. Many lookers but no buyers. Early in the school year, my friend Jil invited Sarikki to stay with her and her son in Zeeland. Rikki and Nate were good friends. My "taxi" duties were reduced a bit. I was so thankful. But I continued to drive Martina back and forth. By Christmas vacation, she was having difficulty adjusting to school in Zeeland. She typed me the following lengthy note on my work computer while she was visiting my office.

"Dear Ms. Forgwe (Mom),

As you know, I am very frustrated. I am frustrated because of the fact that I go to Zeeland Middle School. It is a very depressing school. I don't think that I should have to go to a school where I am not happy. I think that I should look forward to coming to school, and it should be a fun experience, not a miserable one.

If you go to Zeeland, you have to look and act a certain way. You have to be white and have blond hair and blue eyes. If you are any different, it is extremely hard to get accepted. I don't want to be in a school where the standards are set up like that. I want to be in a school where it is a little bit more multi-cultural. I want to be in a school with a little more variety. Zeeland SUCKS! The kids are so stuck up. They are used to growing up in a little country town with nothing but people like them, and as soon as someone different moves in, they can't accept that person.

I think that if I got away for a while and then came back, I would mature a little and learn to deal with Zeeland, or Zeeland would have to learn to deal with me. I'm sure that Uncle Gene and Aunt Mary would be OK with this if you would explain to them how I am suffering. I'm sure they would be very understanding. Joy, please try to understand how I am feeling. Please, put yourself in my shoes. I would really appreciate it if you would give me this opportunity. It would be an excellent learning experience for me. I would learn about other places in the country besides Zeeland. Don't you think that that would be a great learning experience? I definitely think it would be.

I realize that this is going to be one of the hardest decisions that you will ever make, but please try to see things from my viewpoint. Try to think about what would be the best for me. Please, make a wise decision considering what you just read.

Sincerely, Martina Forgwe"

I was torn between insisting that Martina adjust to Zeeland and paving the way for her to leave. She started acting out, making life miserable for us, including herself. In time, my empathy turned into frustration. Afterall, Martina's unhappiness was the reason my house was on the market! I asked my brother, Gene, for help. By spring, I could no longer cope, and Gene and Mary agreed to have Martina stay with them and finish 8th grade in Connecticut.

After months of painting, fixing and repairing, my cute little cape cod home attracted a buyer. In May I purchased a house on Division Street in the small city of Zeeland. When summer arrived, and Martina returned to Michigan from Connecticut, Sarikki and I were already living in Zeeland. I had never considered what living in Zeeland would be like for me. Zeeland was a smaller community than Holland, and even less diverse, if that was possible. In fact, Zeeland was similar to my home town in Iowa, a very tight pocket of Dutch tradition. What was really on my mind was that I didn't like living in such close proximity to Yolanda. But the good news was that my friend, Jil, lived around the block from me, and we had countless occasions to catch up on our life's opportunities and struggles. Our friendship went back many years. We had worked together in the Physics and Astronomy Department at Michigan State in the early 1970's. Jil, like me, had endured a painful marriage that ended in divorce. Both of us were raising our children alone. I was delighted to have the chance to share with Jil.

Martina began her first year of high school in Zeeland. Initially she did quite well, developing some friendships. But similar to her experience in the eighth grade, Martina coped well for only a short period of time. By the end of the school year, she began manipulating everyone to enable her to leave Zeeland.

Martina wrote another letter to her dad. She told Christopher that as far as she was concerned, he was not her father. She told him that *"any boy could make a baby, but it took a real man to raise one."* She told Chris how hard it was for her mother, all alone, and she chastised Chris for rarely writing, calling, etc. She chided him for not answering her last letter. She basically told him she hated him. Surprisingly, Chris answered Martina's letter.

"My Dear Daughter,

Thank you very much for your heart-rending letter which I am sure took lots of inner strength, courage, and forthrightness to write. Some of Fitemi's letters have in the past jolted me into similar tearful sobs and paroxysms, but of late she has been quite gentle with me and many of the tears that flowed when I read her last letters were tears of joy. I wish Bentasi and Sarikki could also take the trouble to say 'hello Christopher' even if they cannot find it within themselves to say 'hello daddy.'

It amazes me so much that you can muster such a heavy blend of gall, sarcasm, and hard-hitting satire just to get your father's attention. You have borne your heart so candidly that in a way I can perceive you (whom I have never seen) much more vividly than I can your two brothers (whom I have hugged and kissed many times over), but whose story is yet to be told. You have every right to be bitter and to scream and claw at me across the Atlantic, but in the end our agony can only be relieved when we take it out on each other (if we must) face to face.

Even if I am the monster I have been made out to be you still deserve and are entitled to the right to determine from up close who your father is, beyond what other people say. It hurts me so much to be referred to as "the aggressor" in a letter written by one of you to my brother after 15 years of not even knowing what has become of me.

You have been denied the chance to get to know your father within the intimate context of family but you must understand that it is not your father who packed his bags and quit the family home. Your father sees himself as the first victim of this ungodly rupture which has plunged him into 15 years of wilderness experience. Part of my anguish comes from knowing the kind of hostility you have to cope with in America simply by being who you are.

Fortunately for you (if I am to believe yours and Fitemi's letters) your mother has proved more than equal to the task of steering you through the jungle of difficulties with all of your faculties intact. One thing is clear to me; you have been having a rough time of it, but the ideas that come through in your letters tell me that you are maturing into a level headed young lady. I thank God and Joy for that.

You were upset by my writing you as if we have been familiar with each other all along. You even scold me for daring to end my letter to you with 'love from your Dad.' Well, God's ideal is for members of the family to love and be tolerant towards each other. It does not always work out that way, but that is no reason not to yearn to attain the ideal.

So I hope you will from now be gracious enough to permit me to indulge in some wishful thinking, and why not some fervent hope, that the day is still

to come when my undying desire to be with you will be satisfied. It is this
hope that enables me to cope with life alone in an apartment with relative
calm and composure. I look forward to reading a 'Dear Father' letter from
my one and only 'Mother Martina.'

Abundant Love from Your Dad

Martina's emotions were pulled and squeezed concerning her father. She wanted to meet him and get to know him, but at the same time, she was very angry with him. Martina worked me very hard – trying to get her way. She told me that it was difficult being one of only two or three black students in Zeeland High. She said she couldn't be herself and that the other students didn't understand her. And those circumstances were true, so it was easy to sympathize with Martina. But Martina had a hard time accepting Martina. It was difficult to know what would be best. I tried to help Martina see that adjusting to her present situation would be the best thing she could do. She became angry with me and tried all the harder to leave.

I continued to cover up my pain by pouring myself into my kids' lives, especially Martina's struggles. Martina wanted me to smooth out the rough spots in her life, and I willingly took on that challenge, probably as a convenient avoidance of my own anguish.

After not much worked out for Martina, she decided that she wanted to visit her father in Cameroon – a desire she confided to her father's sister, Auntie MaryAnn. MaryAnn, now living in Virginia, arranged for a conference call, and Martina talked with her dad over the telephone. Martina was the "perfect little girl" on the phone. I don't know what Chris said to her, but I could tell by the look on Martina's face that it wasn't going to work out for her to go to Cameroon. When Martina hung up the phone, she was livid. She said her dad was stupid. She said he didn't want her to come now but to wait for two or three years. She started crying saying that nobody wanted her, and nobody liked her. Through her tears, Martina moaned that even her dad didn't like her, and he had never met her.

I was darting in many directions while raising four adolescents. While I was trying to help Martina, I was pestered by fears that I might be neglecting Temi, Tasi, and Rikki. I wondered if I was being fair to all four of my kids. Fitemi radiated so much wisdom and competency with all that she attempted to do that it didn't seem she needed too much help from me – and she was an exchange student in France, far away from home. Both Bentasi and Sarikki seemed happy and content, immersed with their respective activities – school, and athletics; and they rarely complained. We should have talked more. Martina was extremely good at letting me know what was bothering her.

But I failed to recognize my own state. I allowed circumstances to drain my energy. My parents were approaching the sunset years, and I was needed to help with their care. I was in pretty bad shape. I abhorred food for its power over me. I felt more inadequate than ever before. Anger built up inside of me – trying to escape – but I couldn't release it; I turned it against myself. I felt like I was going to explode – it was as if I could feel the anger that had been festering for years inside of me.

Instead of moderating my self-defeating behaviors, I increased my dependence on them. I wondered why I had allowed myself to move to Zeeland. Was it really worth it? It was stressful enough to go through the whole house selling and buying thing. And then to top it off, end up in a place I hated more than where I moved from. And what's more, Martina was adjusting no better than she did in Holland!

I was perplexed. I started gaining weight. I smoked more. I stayed in bed as late as possible, whenever possible. A dark, cloudy haze settled over me, blocking out any daylight.

But I routinely rolled out of bed at six a.m. when my overly dependable alarm signaled the day's dreary beginning. I obliviously showered, dressed, and took off for work, hoping to escape the smothering fingers of that damn haze. The five-mile drive from Zeeland to Holland perked up my spirits when I saw the sunrise as I turned onto Chicago Drive from Maple Avenue.

But as I peeked out at the morning colors via my rearview mirror, I felt crippled. Why in the hell was this happening to me? I drove to my job site numerous times only to turn around, drive back home, and crawl into my cozy bed – tucked in by my own private cloud of despair. I became overwhelmed with everything and could deal with nothing. Small errands became insurmountable chores. Oftentimes, I stayed in bed all day.

I was in a state of bewilderment. I neglected myself, my family, my friends, and my responsibilities at work. Depression took hold of me, draining all my energies.

In the midst of my turmoil, I gained about eighty pounds – after I had spent the year before religiously going to Formu-3 Weight Loss Center, where I obtained a certificate for a 100-pound loss! I had never before had such difficulty performing daily tasks. I gave up.

Mom exclaimed how vibrant the autumn leaves were that year, 1994, but I didn't see those colors or that vibrancy. Holding the frayed cord together, I prayed my bargain phone would stay intact long enough for me to place my call. My doctor had referred me to a psychologist in Zeeland. I was ambivalent about going, but I obediently got in my rusty '82 Golf and drove to the counseling office on the corner of State Street and Chicago Drive. The receptionist introduced me to my therapist, and I wondered how such a short, lanky young man could do anything to help me. I thought it was laughable – and finding the humor in anything was difficult. I felt lifeless; I couldn't sense autumn's briskness. Falling leaves signaled the disappearance of summer. I was closer to fifty than forty, and I couldn't pull my dragging bones out of bed. What in the hell was wrong with me?

My therapist and I met for half-hour sessions twice weekly. I talked non-stop, but thirty minutes was barely enough time to get started. After a few meetings, my counselor encouraged me to try writing a journal. His suggestion annoyed me, for I was too damn exhausted to exert any effort. Why couldn't he just do his job? Why did I have to relive all the drama again?

Winter was dismal and unending, complete with an array of problems – disputes among my children, financial difficulties, and many missed workdays. And then came the spring rains. My basement flooded. While rescuing some soggy boxes, I uncovered a beat-up crate full of boxes sealed and taped tightly shut -- filled with letters and paraphernalia from the 60s and 70s. Shuffling through stacks of papers and pictures, I came across some paper scraps! OMG! Reading through those scraps, tears rolled down my cheeks. WTF? What could be the purpose in drudging up all that old stuff? I felt like shit, but at least I was feeling something. Yes, life must be lived by looking forward and embracing the present – but could it be that life can only be understood by looking back? I wanted to understand, so I chose to reverse my hasty decision to never look back. Could it be that my therapist's advice was wise?

But how would I start? I'm not a writer. I'm not even that much of a reader – not because of a lack of interest, but more because of a lack of time – or could it be priorities? With the advice of my therapist pestering my mind, I pondered trying my hand at some journalizing. It was time to free-up the time and find some sharpened pencils and lots of paper.

Grabbing a stack of narrow-lined college notebooks, I walked to Windmill Restaurant and penciled out the words*: "Putting the pieces together is overwhelming; I don't know if I'm ready to do this."* I kept at it, however; spending countless hours sipping coffee, chain smoking, and scribbling out my thoughts in longhand in that quaint little Dutch café. I went there for lunch during the week and for a few hours at the end of each work-day. When I went home after work, after the household duties were completed, sleeping was replaced by editing my jottings and writings and subsequently pounding out their meanings on my keyboard.

I reflected and wrote over many months, bringing up as many thoughts and memories as I could – using as much love, patience, dedication, stamina, and foresight that I could cough up – hopefully coated with a little wisdom and humor.

I felt compelled to tell my story. My journalizing began as a therapeutic exercise, a way to heal myself. And the entries were written decades ago – in the mid-1990s. I was in my late 40's, Fitemi and Bentasi in their 20's, and Sarikki and Martina were still in their teens.

I wanted to share what I had learned, but it wasn't fit to read – not from all those little bits and pieces. It was so chaotic and wordy and messy. I composed that stuff to help me get better – to pull myself out of depression. So I decided to store my journal away, keeping it intact so as to re-work it at a later time. I neatly packed up all its bits and pieces, swearing to return to it at a later date.

In spite of the unorganized and chaotic nature of my original journal writing, the important outcome was that it did its job! As I have enjoyed the return of my self-worth, I have overcome many of my self-defeating behaviors. Writing my journal – in its very messy form – helped me to heal. That healing is portrayed in its various stages throughout my poetry and prose.

CHAPTER 7

Poetry and Prose

I wrote these poems and anecdotes in the mid-1990s – more than fifteen years after I gained the courage to walk away from a decade of mistreatment and debasement, after I reluctantly left behind many friends and dear family members in charming Cameroon, and after I returned to Michigan to begin a new journey with my four children.

I would like to share some of my writings with you -- not because I have any more to share than anyone else, but in a spirit of emboldening people to carve out their own unique journeys – and encouraging an end to silence.

a new day

Cameroon, so far away, spelled freshness and delight
it was for me, so long ago, a beacon in my life
why was I running, fast and scared, what could my eyes not see?
I searched for calmness in my heart midst tropical warm air

what came to me was nothing more than life's grim past abuse
the beauty of the countryside just blanketed my pain
for my first love, he turned on me, he tied me up in knots
and as I shared my life with him, my soul he pulled apart

he frightened me – drew blood and tears; he was a callous man
the chains he tightened, cold & firm; he bound my feet & hands
I can't remember all the things he did to take control
but in my mind, I built a plan – deliverance my goal

he took away the world I knew, what I gave free to him
took back his passion and his love and gave them to my friends
I stood there with my kids – all three – another on her way
I packed my bags, so secretly –

Tomorrow's a New Day

By Joy Klaaren Forgwe, 1995

April 28, 1995

When I left home, I was ill-prepared for many things. I tried to make something happen in my life, but nothing much happened except all the theatrics I created around things not happening! I thought life was a locked door and that other people knew something I didn't. I struggled with overeating since I was a young child. Food became my comfort zone. I think I kept myself out of a lot of situations by padding myself with unwanted pounds, preventing me from participating in some activities. I looked for meaning in my life by throwing myself into studying, getting good grades, and organizing and participating in human and civil rights causes. I even tried to be a flower child in the 60's! Remember the treks to LA?

May 2, 1995

But fulfillment never came. So, I set out to do what my culture taught me – find Mr. Right, get married, have children, and live happily ever after. However, my life didn't actually work out quite like that. I did get married. I did have children. But the "happily ever after" part lay dormant for many years. I had a bumpy past – my first sexual experience, at age 19, was a violent rape; and then I lived through a 10-year mentally, physically and sexually abusive marriage, followed by 20 years of trying to work through tons of intense anger directed towards others and myself, while raising four children by myself.

choices

women have the right to choose I believe this

the movement in my belly was p u l s a t i n g ever so strongly

galloping out the precarious trottings of life—coping & not coping

'midst turmoil and despair I made not a choice to join my soul with his that
night for the splendor, the awe, the delight had been drowned

prematurely buried by the changing tides of first love's promises and
commitments drenched in a sea of lies, lust and abandonment

Then I fell in love with the exquisite babe stirring in my womb

For she moved impetuously; her first awakenings were like a sign gently
bobbing me across the Chari River beginning calmly as a soothing stream
then transforming dramatically into a wild current

Treading impatiently yearning to burst over her banks to flood us all with
spontaneity with enthusiasm and with the waves of reality

We have chosen to discover each other

By Joy Klaaren Forgwe, 1995

May 8, 1995

People search and search for meaning in many ways and in many things. There's a lot of talk these days about good old-fashioned family values. Many politicians, evangelists, and general do-gooders are espousing a return to "the good old days." What exactly does all this talk mean — were these "old values" in place when America destroyed the Native Americans, and promoted slavery in order to build all kinds of massive economic gains? To return to a time when the "old values" were in place is to return to a time when Native Americans were dying by the thousands, it is to return to a time when Africans were slaves, when immigrants from Mexico, Guatemala, Ireland, Venezuela, Vietnam, Iraq, and many other countries in Southeast Asia, the Middle East, Central America and South America were treated grossly unfairly, when women were heavily oppressed, and when America sought a homogeneity that denied the reality of God's creation. Those times were times when diversity was negated. To return to that time is to return to the evil days of this nation. America was built on the blood of our sisters and brothers — the Native Americans — a painful past that many of us have not come to terms with.

May 9, 1995

People are now more able to speak out. What matters to many of us is not material wealth and success, but peace of mind, and general well-being. The key is not homogeneity, but learning to work together.

Violence — guns, drugs, aggression and racism — is a response to our refusal to appreciate and accept and love people for who they are.

We would be wise to choose to be happy together. We would be wise to learn to work together, glorying in our diversity. These are not the old values.

May 10, 1995

What makes a woman so dependent on a man – in particular, so stuck in a no-win relationship? For centuries women have been misrepresented. We were taught to throw ourselves at a man. If we didn't have one hooked by the time we were out of high school, we could always enroll in college. And when we married, our man was supposed to be our life! The woman who does not see and feel her own inherent worth easily becomes dependent on someone else. This is so unbalanced – out of whack with the natural scheme of things. Many of today's religions preach this imbalance! It's sad that many women are selling themselves short. There's so much to learn and enjoy. It's impossible to study philosophy and religion and history without becoming irate concerning the profound distortions of women. Why can't women just blossom? Why do we have to extinguish our own flames in order to let someone else shine? Where does all this repression and self-hatred come from? With no positive self-concept, a woman is empty and merely sparkles and glitters (if even that) – a welcome vessel for others' projections.

craving

I crave writing

to pour out meaning-filled thoughts from the pieces left dangling from my spirit

yes the words come not with a fresh style, not with the latest fashion, not with untouched freedom and latitude

but with the choking sins of yesterday

the fabric of today's ponderings is sharply tattered, lacerated from the moisture of crushing changes sprung on my cavalcade of free-spirited jollity and play

mirage against mirage, fists against the glass, deflecting my fingers from whispering in the wind

I have lost parts of myself, and I crave loquaciousness

By Joy Klaaren Forgwe, 1995

May 16, 1995

An old song I used to sing in Sunday School as a small child just flashed into my mind:

> *Red and Yellow, Black and White,*
> *They are precious in God's sight,*
> *Jesus loves the little children of the world.*

Familiar words to a familiar song, yet not so familiar that we are continually impacted by their meaning. The simple truth revealed in these words is that, yes, we are all different – different colors, different races, different ethnic backgrounds. And with all of our differences, Jesus loves us.

No, wait. That's not what the song says. It doesn't say that Jesus loves US; it says that Jesus loves the LITTLE CHILDREN!

There is more than just simple truth in this melody. Jesus loves the little children, all the children of the world, because somehow, in their beautiful innocence, they look at each other without bias, without feelings of superiority, and without criticism. As a world full of oppression and hate revolves ever so violently around a child's small slice of naiveté that we might call heaven, these children laugh and play and experience the newness of life with other children around them, be they red, yellow, black, or white.

Of course, this is before they become old enough to learn that the world, and yes, even the church, doesn't really value the message taught in that Sunday School song.

May 29, 1995

A joyful spirit is an important ingredient for happiness, for one of life's biggest handicaps is a bad attitude. But exuberance for living still has to come from grasping what it means to be alive -- which has taken me floods of tears and hundreds of pages of writing and decades of talking and searching. In fact, I rarely keep quiet or sit still. I can't seem to stop thinking and writing. Loving others necessitates difficult things like tolerance and forgiveness – and endless understanding. But loving others yields endless blessings.

I wish that I had been more aware, when my children were babies, of what I now have come to realize by observing them over the last two decades:

We were born with perfect programming.
We began life with love, and then we learned fear.
Love is inside of us, and it cannot be destroyed.

I recalled Dad telling me that the most important thing to pray for was to ask God to help us love others as much as God loves us. Wow – so simple, yet so profound!

June 18, 1995

By saying that I will make things work out by myself, I'm simply acknowledging that no one else is going to do it for me. But at the same time, I am aware that my life is directed by a force in the universe that is much greater than myself. I believe the greatest underlying force in the world is love – love of myself – and love for each other.

June 20, 1995

Take the time to get rid of any superficial debris you've been enculturated into. Examine all the things you have taken for granted. You may be wise to discard some things you look at as necessities. But also take time to think things through before throwing out everything that you hate just because it's what you were taught. Don't throw out the good with the bad. Some things you were taught have value. They just need to be viewed from a different perspective.

June 21, 1995

I'm shedding myself of the past. It isn't healthy to drag around a ton of anger. I've made a conscious decision to put the past behind me, now that I've gained understanding and freedom from my many decades of silence — secured by my journalizing and writing.

I can now see that I was ripe for being abused. The people who misled and deceived me should not be entirely blamed for the whole pattern of events — neither should they be excused; but if I had cared more about myself, I could have reduced some of my past pain. The people who hurt and deceived me were dealing with their own hurts and troubles and circumstances. I harbor no hatred toward any of them — in fact, I wish for them to feel joy and love and forgiveness. Coming to terms with the past will help them encounter happiness.

June 22, 1995

I've worn myself out working on dissolving my anger. I've lived with it, repressed it, and feebly tried to express it. I want to be done with it! I think it's starting to dissipate. However, I still feel the pain. The pain will never go away. But I am more aware of who Joy is — in the present.

My perspective on life and the world would not be what it is today if I had not experienced all that I have lived and struggled through. I now have a pretty good outlook on life. Possessions are not important to me.

Relationships are important. Forgiveness is important. Respect is important. Even fun is important. But love is the most important of all.

I'm feeling better about myself. Maybe I'm a tad smarter than I think I am. I'm trying to get my priorities straight.

July 2, 1995

I don't wish to be a victim of other people's unwise, unloving acts. I know I can't change other people, but I can look at situations differently.

I don't want to be judgmental. I don't want to close my heart. My perceptions change when I make an effort to love and understand.

July 7, 1995

 My house is often overflowing with teenagers. They drop by in little groups from noon to midnight, seven days a week. Sometimes I wish I lived in the country – so all the cars arriving and departing wouldn't bother anyone. I think my neighbors are sometimes annoyed with all the "goings-on." I love it – but I don't wish to disturb anyone. There's really no place for young people to hang out – where they can be themselves.

Joys

bursting in and out of here with tales of far-off places I just don't feel like
quality mothering today

her toothbrush is dripping onto the floor while the
tattered shower curtain hangs all disheveled as too many folks monopolize
my bathroom

and those dishes are piling up

her world has grown broader while mine is just trying to
keep up, hang on, with all those new perspectives and boarders

I just want to know if she's growing closer to herself and
maybe even to me

why is it we can barely stand to be in the same room

she acts, I react

I act, she reacts

parent and child – child and parent

we both want to gallop while we live through each other's frustrations

frosted with idealistic anticipation of what life could be

should be

is

just dealing with our spontaneity

the reality of it all

last night she slept next to her mommy like a newborn babe suckling up to the warmth of the one who brought her into this world, birthed her 'midst all the fray friends and family could deal out

yes I always do just as I please, at least what my heart tells me to do, so how are we any different?

parading the edges, bleak borders in time

our wants pull us this way and that way — detached

two souls trying to love themselves, trying to fit into a world of conflict and unfair games and just stark reality

two souls of the same lineage vine trying to stamp out mediocrity

we've always had trouble running in the margins set

alike yet different

mother and daughter

much the same

reaching out, holding back

tears, laughter, shouting

hugging, crying, dancing

living, loving, growing

Joy Beth and Martina Joy

By Joy Klaaren Forgwe

(written for Mother & Daughter)

July 21, 1995

My style of parenting is relaxed yet firm, suggestive yet flexible, and non-judgmental. I strive to provide an atmosphere which promotes sharing and constructive learning and decision-making. I listen carefully, gather as much info as possible, and trust my children to do what's right for them.

Many of my friends and family members think I'm too lenient. I don't want to be controlling. I refuse to direct them; they must direct themselves.

August 9, 1995

I have faith in my children. They may not choose paths I think are wise, but the choices they make will be their own choices. And they will fail and succeed over and over again. They will learn, sooner or later. I will always support them and I will always love them – unconditionally.

August 20, 1995

I enjoy the lighter side of life – catching pieces of just plain old fun. Last night I played cards; games have always been entertaining for me. They are kind of soothing. And they can bring out the best in folks. I remember when I taught MaryAnn some American games – Rummy, Pounce, Euchre, Monopoly, Scrabble. I learned some Cameroonian games – James Bond, Cassava, etc. They called clubs "black cassava;" and diamonds "four corners." Those were wonderful exchanges.

August 29, 1995

My bank account is a disaster! I just took out a loan to pay overdue bills. When my money runs out – and my checks start to bounce, I get anxious, for I don't know how I'll settle my obligations. When I feel this way, I thank God for the blessings that I have.

September 3, 1995

My children are beautiful young people.

Martina has an incredible amount of energy. She rises early daily and is off to school by 6 a.m. Martina has a very perceptive mind, predicting what people will say or do. Her writing skills are far ahead of her 16 years. She's creative and spontaneous.

Sarikki is well-liked by everyone. He attracts multitudes of friends all hours of the day and night. At age 17, Sarikki is a very unselfish young man, having the ability to make everyone feel accepted and welcomed and loved. He excels as an athlete, yet he always remembers he is part of a team

Bentasi, named after the wisest man in the village of Njindom, is an amicable laid-back 21-year-old philosopher. He loves to discuss issues, always expounding thoughtfully and in a mild manner. Bentasi, quite a smooth operator, likes to search for the underlying meaning in everything. He's fun to be around, accepting of all people.

Fitemi has incredible drive and determination; and she is very intelligent. Fitemi is fluent in Spanish and French; and she's used her linguistic skills to travel the world. Fitemi is an international person, with a passion for different cultures and peoples. At 24, she's seen more of this globe than most people experience in a lifetime.

September 11, 1995

Today Fitemi and I had lunch at Abbie's Alley Restaurant in the small conservative town of Zeeland. I could feel the stares. I don't have too much trouble ignoring the rubbernecks, but nonetheless, it has its draining effects. Some things take their toll on you without you even noticing. I never experienced much discrimination in Cameroon – just a happiness with the fact that we were "unusual."

It seems harder to be "different" in this country. There is more pressure to fit in – for everyone to be the same – act the same, have the same values, dress the same, look the same. It's a diverse, global world – getting more so every day. My children have a lot of things to bear, but they will be better equipped to deal with the world as it grows closer and closer.

September 30, 1995

In the outside world, Fitemi, Bentasi, Sarikki and Martina have to watch every step they take. Their skin color oftentimes throws them into encounters with bias and ignorance. It's as if they have to be entirely honest, kind, smart – never making any mistakes. All I could do was to bring them up in a loving home. I've done my best. I hope none of my children become bitter. I pray they take the attitude of working to realize their dreams, in spite of others' perceptions and prejudices.

October 20, 1995

I feel like things are starting to come together for me. My happy spirit is present more often than months ago. I feel I have a handle on my anger – I can talk about it without getting so defensive. My attitude concerning myself and my kids is much more optimistic than when I started writing. I've worked through some emotions that I had never before dared to look at.

Love is about the only thing in this world that's real.

October 25, 1995

I have always had a vision for my life – to live life fully, to use all my potential, to be creative, to treat everyone respectfully, to have a joyful spirit, and to be trusting and loving. But never in all my dreaming did I foresee trust ending in rape, or love ending in deception. I became disillusioned and I short-circuited myself by squelching my potential and allowing my bad habits to control me.

October 27, 1995

I have learned a lot. I'm compulsive and very obsessive. And I demand a lot of myself, and others. I'm definitely more active than passive. I'm also quite diplomatic – oftentimes assuming the role of a peacemaker – which leads me to one of my most troubling faults. I think my biggest flaw is that I'm not confrontational; I cringe at negatives – I definitely like the sun to shine. To continue on a bright note, I like to live life with a certain flair! I possess a high dose of tolerance and strength. I am a loving and tender person. I'm a cheerful person. I feel whole. I feel complete. I'm bubbling over with a joyful spirit, and I want to share my enthusiasm

November 1, 1995

    My self-defeating behaviors probably served some purpose initially — for I'm still around; unfortunately, they are now glued to me, clouding my eyesight. But I never lost sight of my vision. My love of life continued to grow, even though not every part was always blooming — living life fully was sometimes difficult as I tried to make sense of an unfair and un-loving world. Life was not as cozy and comfortable as when I picked corn with my high school classmates, rode horses on Holstein's farm, or edited the class yearbook in Sioux Center. There have been many surprises — from ardent brutality and domination to encounters with people who didn't think and became dangerously caught up in the cosmetics of life.

November 25, 1995

    As I matured, I realized there were always more things to learn and more burdens to endure; I also realized that there were endless experiences to enjoy. Yes, life has its hurdles, and I often buried my dreams, getting caught up in the details of existing. Do not lose sight of life's charm. Living fully takes energy, endurance, and love -- and a proper dose of plain old fun! Hanging in there bears rich fruit — the rewards of embracing life, in all its splendor, flow daily if you just tune in your senses — from each stunning sunrise to each kind deed to each tear dried to each friendship cultivated. Relationships are vital to me; they entail hard work and honesty and understanding. I wish I had an endless supply of energy.

November 28, 1995

Society teaches you to conform – but if you do, you will be overwhelmed with life's unfairness. I recommend a healthy questioning of everything you take for granted. The only preparation for tomorrow is the wise use of today. I've learned that honesty is the first step in dealing with shortcomings. I have some addictions that are running my life. Do I want to continue to be controlled?

December 2, 1995

Forgiveness. I must not punish myself for every stupid decision I've made, self-defeating habit I've developed, or unwise choice I've put into action. Forgiveness is the forerunner of strength. Couple a forgiving spirit with a loving one, and pour it all into your relationships. Have fun. Think about what you're doing. Learn. Be flexible. Be tolerant. Fight against prejudice and stereotyping. Love, unconditionally. Be careful who you look up to. You can see God in everyone if you look deep enough.

December 8, 1995

Life has been an opportunity for me. I've enjoyed life in many places, including Cameroon – an experience which changed my life. I now live in the U.S.A., and I know that here in America I have the luxury to enjoy certain freedoms: freedom of choice, including career, where to live, who to be with (family, and other social groups), who to love, what faith or religion to practice, and on and on. But these freedoms are not enjoyed equally by everyone. I feel driven to combat injustice, for freedom implies responsibility, commitment, morality – which are all too often lacking – buried under the "curse" to get ahead, be successful, and acquire endless possessions and power.

December 12, 1995

I can't put my finger on the reason, but I feel a lot better. I've been more excited about life. It's easier for me to have a good time. Yet feeling better doesn't mean I'm happy all the time; in fact, I've been sad a lot lately — so sad that I've caught myself crying at the strangest times.

I can feel a shift in my life — even before it happens. I know, because I've been on the verge of tears numerous times this week. I want to cry. I need to cry. I just haven't been able to let go. Every time I'm close to tears, I end up laughing. Yes, I'm the one who's always jolly, always upbeat, always cheerful and polite and nice (damn, I hate that word "nice") to everyone. I'm good at making jokes about my life. I jest about Christopher's abuse. I quip about his many affairs. I laugh at people's impertinence. When do I cry? Well, I'm crying now — even as I write these words. I'm weeping about my past terror, and I'm weeping about how I turned on myself.

Just as I left Christopher, I am telling myself to begin another exodus. I will stop battering myself. I am choosing to love myself, to forgive myself for many unwise choices, and to be happy.

December 12, 1995

The greatest possession I have is the 24 hours in front of me. I can't win if I don't begin. Writing these journal and diary entries has been a great beginning. I've worked hard, and I'm proud of that.

Recalling the not-so-pleasant past has been difficult. It has opened doors that I had tightly closed — and I feel rejuvenated. I have gained a lot. Life can only be understood by looking backward — but I know that life must be lived by looking forward and embracing the present.

December 17, 1995

I commit myself to taking better care of Joy. When I crossed the Chari River in 1979 for a new beginning, I did not realize all that I would have to face.

I now realize that there were, and are, and always will be, many rivers to cross. I've tried my best to navigate those rivers with a sense of joy and wisdom — for there are many more things I want to do and enjoy.

I want to see my children grow and find purpose and happiness, and I want to have lots of grandchildren and great-grandchildren to love unconditionally and enjoy enthusiastically.

I see myself now as a pretty strong, intelligent, and loving person. But I need more energy! I possess a pretty good dose of stamina, but I yearn for even more fortitude and vigor. Why? Because I love life.

December 22, 1995

Last night, I received the most joyous news in the world! Fitemi gave birth to a beautiful baby girl – Canelle Joy !!! My first grandchild! WOW! I hope to have many more.

Life is great. Life is beautiful. Life goes on ….. I'm flying high …

Somehow, I'll find a way to gain more stamina! There are so many things I want to do.

What's happening to me?

I feel calmer. I feel good.

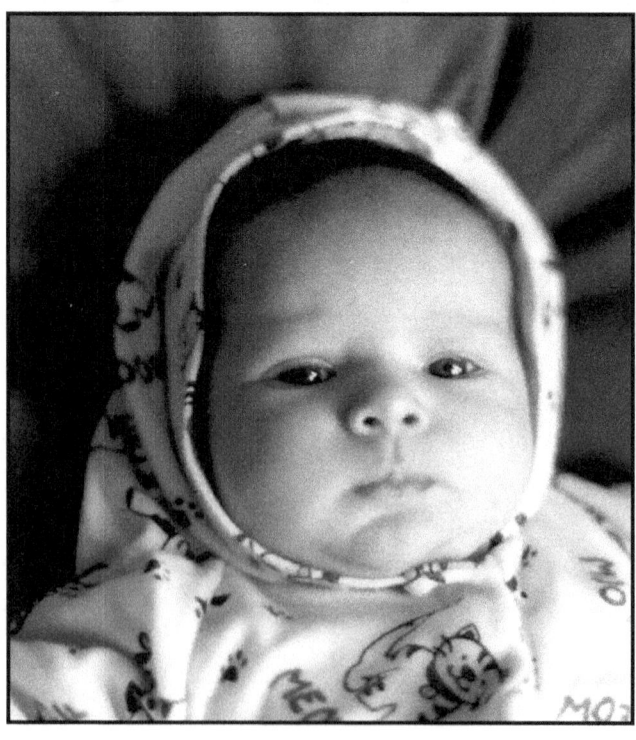

CANELLE 1995

CHAPTER 8

Choosing Joy

As I moved into my mid to late 70s, I dug out the crate with my boxed-up therapeutic journal writings – for I had promised myself to one-day re-work and re-write my journal. That day appeared -- and I began morphing all that old messy stuff into this memoir, <u>Crossing the Chari River</u>. I have gained peace by forgiving myself, recognizing my stamina, and ending my silence.

Silence, if not ended, will turn into anger, frustration, and depression – which can make it impossible to cope with life's challenges. I know this, for it happened to me.

By writing down many of my thoughts thirty-some years ago and then returning to it recently, I was able to look back at a life which had been blanketed with a festering silence about rape and abuse – memories I did not want to share. Writing enabled me to heal.

Fitemi, Bentasi, Sarikki, and Martina got caught right in the midst of my silence – and also my gloom and misery. They have had their ups and downs, and they will have additional ups and downs – but they have all blossomed and matured and are in healthy scenarios of their own; I could not be prouder of each one of them and all of their children – my precious grandchildren.

The writing of this book has been my looking back. I have worked tirelessly over many decades to put all the pieces together – from scribblings on countless paper scraps to jotting down thoughts in old diaries to hundreds of pages of journal entries, trying to understand my choices – some wise and many not-so-wise.

I have looked back at my wholesome upbringing in Iowa, where it all began and where I was grounded in a loving and caring family. I have looked back to my college days, to the tumultuous rape I lived through, to my relationship with Christopher from the soft beginnings to the abusive episodes to the inevitable endings. All of this I have gone over and over in my mind.

Writing enabled me to confront many of my unwise decisions. It's a useful tool for self-examination. I learned a lot about myself by reading and re-reading what I wrote.

I want to thank my mom for encouraging me to keep all my old letters, diaries, and greeting cards. They contained many of the descriptive details which enabled me to compose this memoir.

At times, I have said too much, and at other times, I have not said enough. Sharing memorable slices of my life often brought me to tears, yet many more life experiences brought delight and great pleasure.

I'm thrilled to have regained the positive emotions that lived and bloomed in me as a child – love, gratitude, hope, pride, and, of course, joy.

Epilogue **2025**

I have been blessed. After I looked back at my life through a lot of writing and a lot of work, I met Frank Ortiz in 1998. We decided to spend the rest of our lives together, and we married in 2005 -- when I was 57 and Frank was 61. We enjoy life in a loving, reciprocal, respectful relationship. Both of us have been through some rough times, but in our youthful senior years of 77 and 81, we still have enough spunk left in us to create good times for ourselves and our families and friends.

Frank has four children, and just like me, he has two daughters and two sons. Together, we have eight children, eighteen grandchildren, and two great-grandchildren.

I gave to Frank, and Frank gave to me, the gifts of being loving and understanding and forgiving – of each other and of ourselves.

The garden I dreamed about while I was in Chad has become a reality. Gardening and writing have replaced many of my self-defeating behaviors. Our garden is breathtaking – designed and built by Frank. We maintain and enjoy our "little piece of heaven" together. We will celebrate our 20th anniversary this year – 2025 – and we both feel like we met just yesterday.

FAMILY PHOTOS THROUGH THE YEARS

The Klaaren Family in 1948

Cornelia (Mom), Mary Ann, Eugene, Joy, Marion (Dad)

Keith

Eugene
Mary Ann

The
Klaarens

Keith
Joy Beth

1958

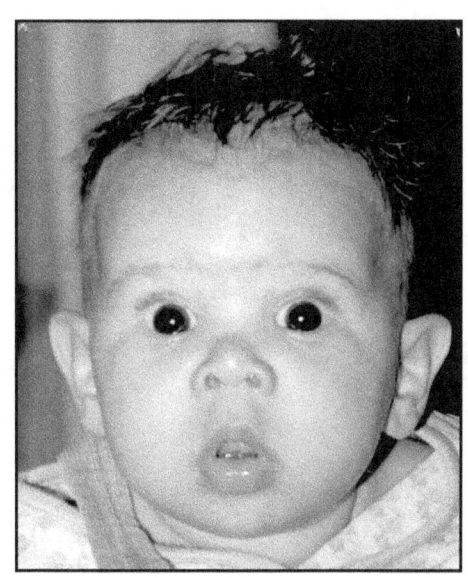

BENTASI, 1974

FITEMI, 1974

Bentasi and Fitemi in 1977,
just before moving to Cameroon.

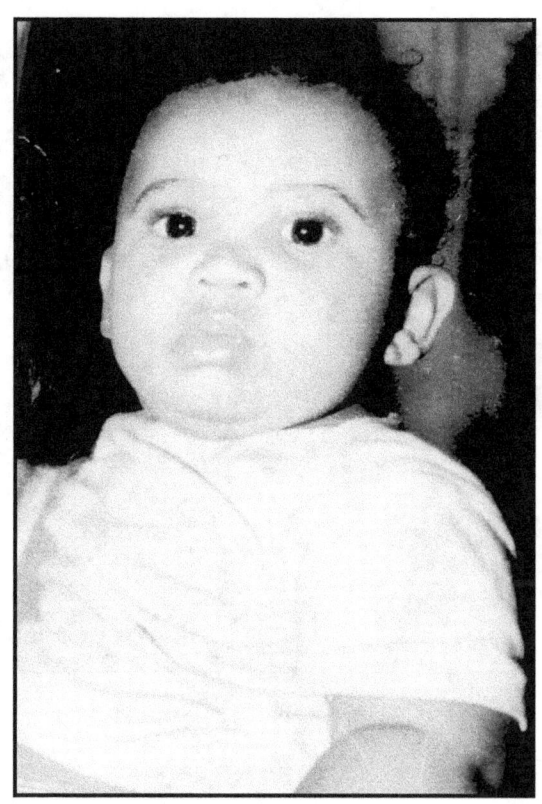

Sarikki, 1978

Sarikki, Mama Forgwe, Papa Forgwe -- 1979

FITEMI, MARTINA, BENTASI, SARIKKI 1979

MARTINA AND GRANDMA KLAAREN 1979

Evolving in the
60's, 70's, 80's & 90's

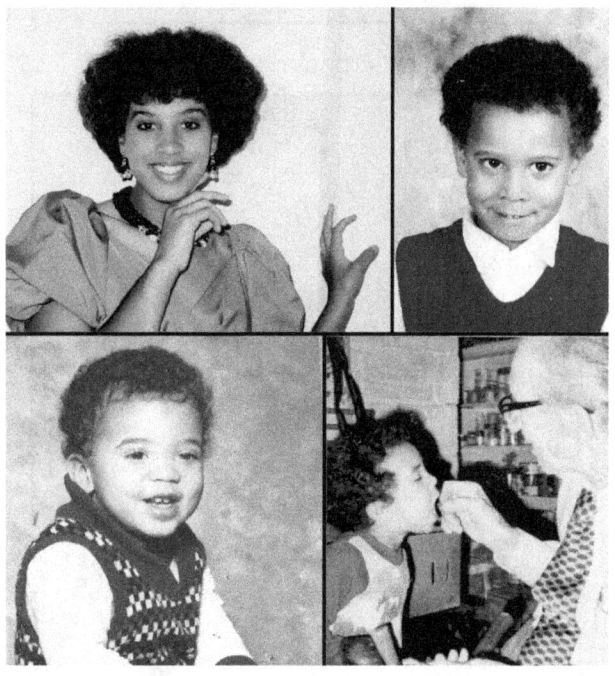

Fitemi, 1981

Sarikki, Fitemi
Martina, Joy, Bentasi
1986

Fitemi, Bentasi
Sarikki, Martina
Mid to late 1990's

www.ingramcontent.com/pod-product-compliance
Lightning Source LLC
Chambersburg PA
CBHW061753120626
46550CB00005B/1979